The Funniest People in Art: 250 Anecdotes

David Bruce

Published by David Bruce, 2022.

While every precaution has been taken in the preparation of this book, the publisher assumes no responsibility for errors or omissions, or for damages resulting from the use of the information contained herein.

THE FUNNIEST PEOPLE IN ART: 250 ANECDOTES

First edition. September 5, 2022.

Copyright © 2022 David Bruce.

ISBN: 979-8215312537

Written by David Bruce.

Table of Contents

Dedication

Dedicated to Carl Eugene Bruce and Josephine Saturday Bruce

My father, Carl Eugene Bruce, died on 24 October 2013. He used to work for Ohio Power, and at one time, his job was to shut off the electricity of people who had not paid their bills. He sometimes would find a home with an impoverished mother and some children. Instead of shutting off their electricity, he would tell the mother that she needed to pay her bill or soon her electricity would be shut off. He would write on a form that no one was home when he stopped by because if no one was home he did not have to shut off their electricity.

The best good deed that anyone ever did for my father occurred after a storm that knocked down many power lines. He and other linemen worked long hours and got wet and cold. Their feet were freezing because water got into their boots and soaked their socks. Fortunately, a kind woman gave my father and the other linemen dry socks to wear.

My mother, Josephine Saturday Bruce, died on 14 June 2003. She used to work at a store that sold clothing. One day, an impoverished mother with a baby clothed in rags walked into the store and started shoplifting in an interesting way: The mother took the rags off her baby and dressed the infant in new clothing. My mother knew that this mother could not afford to buy the clothing, but she helped the mother dress her baby and then she watched as the mother walked out of the store without paying.

***

The doing of good deeds is important. As a free person, you can choose to live your life as a good person or as a bad person. To be a good person, do good deeds. To be a bad person, do bad deeds. If you do good deeds, you will become good. If you do bad deeds, you will become bad. To become the person you want to be, act as if you already are that kind of person. Each of us chooses what kind of person we will become. To become a good person, do the things a good person does. To become a bad person, do the things a bad person does. The opportunity to take action to become the kind of person you want to be is yours.

Human beings have free will. According to the Babylonian Niddah 16b, whenever a baby is to be conceived, the Lailah (angel in charge of contraception) takes the drop of semen that will result in the conception and asks God, "Sovereign of the Universe, what is going to be the fate of this drop? Will it develop into a robust or into a weak person? An intelligent or a stupid person? A wealthy or a poor person?" The Lailah asks all these questions, but it does not ask, "Will it develop into a righteous or a wicked person?" The answer to that question lies in the decisions to be freely made by the human being that is the result of the conception.

A Buddhist monk visiting a class wrote this on the chalkboard: "EVERYONE WANTS TO SAVE THE WORLD, BUT NO ONE WANTS TO HELP MOM DO THE DISHES." The students laughed, but the monk then said, "Statistically, it's highly unlikely that any of you will ever have the opportunity to run into a burning orphanage and rescue an infant. But, in the smallest gesture of kindness — a warm smile, holding the door for the person behind you, shoveling the driveway of the elderly person next door — you have committed an act of immeasurable profundity, because to each of us, our life is our universe."

In her book titled *I Have Chosen to Stay and Fight*, comedian Margaret Cho writes, "I believe that we get complimentary snack-size portions of the afterlife, and we all receive them in a different way." For Ms. Cho, many of her snack-size portions of the afterlife come in hip hop music. Other people get different snack-size portions of the afterlife, and we all must be on the lookout for them when they come our way. And perhaps doing good deeds and experiencing good deeds are snack-size portions of the afterlife.

Cover Artwork for *The Funniest People in Art*:
Copyright by Haiden Fouch, the artist
Used by permission

***

All anecdotes have been retold in my own words to avoid plagiarism.

Most of the anecdotes in this collection are funny, although some are thought provoking rather than funny.

Do you know a language other than English? If you do, I give you permission to translate this book, copyright your translation, publish or self-publish it, and keep all the royalties for yourself. (Do give me credit, of course, for the original book.)

Chapter 1: From Activism to Clothing

Activism

• In 2006, South Dakota instituted an almost total ban on abortions. Bill Napoli, a South Dakota State Senator, supported this ban, saying that women should not be allowed to have abortions even if they get pregnant for "simple rape." (He did say that he would make an exception for a religious virgin who gets pregnant from a brutalizing rape.) Cartoonist Stephanie McMillan saw Mr. Napoli's words as expressing a belief that women shouldn't be allowed to make decisions for themselves, so she created a cartoon in which a woman character telephones Mr. Napoli when she is asked to make a decision about which salad dressing to use — the character asks Mr. Napoli, "Roasted pepper vinaigrette or honey mustard?" The cartoon included Mr. Napoli's work and home telephone numbers, which many other women used to call him. One woman asked him whether her bra and panties should match; another woman asked him whether she should use tampons or pads.[1]

• Fashion maven Sunny Chapman used to go to abortion clinics to protest — as a member of Satanists 4 Life — along with fellow activists Karen Elliott and Monika LaVey. At their *demon*-strations they wore devil horns and devil costumes and held signs saying such things as "DON'T ABORT YOUR FETUS — IT COULD BE THE ANTI-CHRIST" and "PRO-LIFE IS PRO-SATAN." This usually made ordinary pro-life protesters uncomfortable enough to leave the immediate vicinity.[2]

• New York City's Guerrilla Girls use posters to protest art exhibits dominated by male artists. One poster asked, "When Racism & Sexism Are No Longer Fashionable, What Will Your Art Collection Be Worth?" True artists, the Guerilla Girls dress up in gorilla masks to gain publicity for their cause.[3]

• Absolut Vodka once asked lesbian cartoonist Kris Kovick to draw a cartoon to be used in its ads. She drew a cartoon for "Absolut Hurl," which depicted a woman vomiting while holding a vodka bottle. Not surprisingly, Absolut Vodka decided not to use the cartoon in its ads.[4]

Advertising

• In many ways, Theodor Geisel, who is better known as Dr. Seuss, was a lucky man. In the 1920s, he created a cartoon for the humor magazine *Judge*. The cartoon showed a knight in armor lying in bed while a ferocious dragon hovered above him. The caption of the cartoon has the knight referring to a then-common insecticide called Flit: "Darn it all, another Dragon. And just after I'd sprayed the entire castle with Flit!" This cartoon resulted in a contract for Mr. Geisel to create advertisements for Flit because Grace Cleaves saw the cartoon at a hairdresser's shop, liked it, and convinced her husband, a Flit advertising executive, to hire Mr. Geisel. How lucky was Mr. Geisel? When creating the cartoon, he could have used two insecticides: Flit or Fly Tox. He flipped a coin to decide which to use, and Flit won. In addition, Mrs. Cleaves' regular hairdresser's shop did not have *Judge*. Because her regular hairdresser's shop was busy, she went to another hairdresser's shop, where she saw the issue of *Judge* that contained Mr. Geisel's cartoon.[5]

• In 1934, artist Salvador Dalí designed a window that featured nude mannequins for New York department store Bonwit Teller. Of course, the professional window dressers preferred mannequins wearing the clothing that the store sold, so when Mr. Dalí left, they put clothing on the mannequins. When Mr. Dalí returned and saw the alterations to his window display, he made a major display of temperament, including throwing a bathtub used in the display through a plate-glass store window so that the bathtub made an unscheduled stop on the Fifth Avenue sidewalk. Shortly afterward, Mr. Dalí made an unscheduled stop in jail. According to world-famous window dresser Simon Doonan, this situation was win-win for everybody. Mr. Dalí further increased his reputation as an eccentric art genius and the store received lots of fabulous free publicity.[6]

• Surrealist artist Salvador Dalí was outrageous. He once greeted reporters while waving a loaf of bread — which was eight feet long — over his head. He also once wore a tuxedo to a public event — a close look at the tuxedo revealed numerous artificial flies pinned to it. Another time, he arrived in a Rolls-Royce for the opening of an exhibition — the car was filled with cauliflowers. In 1936, he began to give a talk while dressed in an airtight underwater diving suit. Unfortunately, this stunt nearly resulted in his death. He wasn't able to breathe, and it took his audience some time to figure out what was wrong and get his diving helmet off. What kind of art did such a man create? An old Cadillac forms part of a work of art called *Rainy Taxi* — put a coin in a slot and rain falls *inside* the Cadillac.[7]

• R. Crumb's "Keep on Truckin'" drawing became omnipresent during the late 1960s and early 1970s. As so often happens, business later tried to co-opt what was once considered avant garde and controversial. Toyota wished to pay Mr. Crumb lots of money so it could use the drawing and its characters in advertisements for its vehicles. However, Mr. Crumb was unwilling to let Toyota use that particular drawing, suggesting instead that it use a drawing of a headless woman being stuffed into the trunk of a Toyota. Unfortunately, Toyota disliked that idea.[8]

• A marble cutter once took advantage of an unusual opportunity for an advertisement. On his deceased wife's grave monument, he carved, "Here lies Jane Smith, wife of Thomas Smith, marble cutter. This monument was erected by her husband as a tribute to her memory and a specimen of his work. Monuments of the same style 350 dollars."[9]

• Dr. Seuss always said that he couldn't draw, and therefore his drawings were always filled with "exaggerated mistakes." While working as a commercial artist creating drawings for advertisements, he drew a goat that an ad representative thought was a duck. Dr. Seuss then drew a duck — the ad representative thought it was a goat.[10]

AIDS

• The very first panel in the NAMES Project AIDS Memorial Quilt commemorated Marvin Feldman, whose best friend was Cleve Jones, founder of the Names Project. Mr. Jones was despondent following the death of Mr. Feldman. One afternoon he and a friend were in a garage talking about the friends they had lost to AIDS, and as they talked, they painted names and designs upon some fabric. This was therapeutic, so Mr. Jones invited other people to help create a quilt of panels commemorating people who had died of AIDS. Today, the NAMES Project AIDS Memorial Quilt is the largest collectively created work of art in the world.[11]

• While studying at the School of Visual Arts in Manhattan, Keith Haring used to create art on long lengths of paper — the paper was so long that he rolled it out the door and onto the city sidewalk. Passersby used to talk to him about his art. Mr. Haring later said, "Most of them weren't the type to go to art galleries, but a lot of their comments struck me as more perceptive than those of my teachers and fellow students." In 1990, Mr. Haring died of AIDS.[12]

Animals

• Rosebud, the pet cat of children's book author (and artist) Tom Wharton, enjoyed a good book. She liked to sit on whatever book Mr. Wharton was reading, so after a while, Mr. Wharton started giving her books of her own to sit on — *Moby Dick*, *Puss in Boots*, etc. For a couple of years, she sat happily on *Gone With the Wind* as Mr. Wharton read another book. Being a cat, she was a slow reader. Mr. Wharton turned the page for her only every couple of days.[13]

• Navajo artist R.C. Gorman used to keep several pets, including a de-scented skunk, several iguanas, and a pig at his art gallery. However, the skunk and iguanas frightened his models, so he gave these pets to the Albuquerque Zoo. Unfortunately, his pet pig disappeared under suspicious circumstances shortly before a pig barbeque was held near his art gallery.[14]

• To illustrate his Caldecott Medal-winning picture-book, *Make Way for Ducklings*, Robert McCloskey needed to know what the underside of a duck's bill looked like in flight. Therefore, Mr. McCloskey brought a live duck home, wrapped it in a towel, and put it on a couch in such a way that its head stuck out. Mr. McCloskey then lay underneath the duck's head and sketched what he saw.[15]

• Buick, the pet dog of friends of children's book illustrator Tim Lewis, loved cows, and whenever the friends were driving in the country, if someone mentioned the word "cow," Buick would tear around, going from window to window until he sighted the cow. This was hazardous, so eventually the family started spelling the word "cow" when they drove in the country with Buick.[16]

• Like many creative people, Theodor Geisel, who is better known as Dr. Seuss, went through an impoverished period early in life. He and a friend once rented a rat-infested apartment in Greenwich Village. They used canes to drive the rats away from their apartment before going to bed so the rats would not bother them while they were asleep.[17]

• When he was a small boy, Quaker artist Benjamin West made brushes out of hairs from his family's pet cat, but he had to stop doing this after his father noticed that the cat looked as if it had been severely attacked by moths.[18]

• In New York City, comedian Bob Smith worked as a cater-waiter for a woman who introduced her dogs to him by saying, "This is Picasso, and this is Gorky — *the painter, not the writer*."[19]

Architects

• After the 1906 San Francisco earthquake, which destroyed most of the city, architect Julia Morgan was hired to rebuild the Fairmont Hotel, in part because of her expertise in reinforced concrete, which was at that time a new material. Women architects were rare, so a woman reporter inspected the Fairmont Hotel and then asked the foreman, "Is the building really in the charge of a woman architect?" The foreman replied, "This building is in [the] charge of a *real* architect, and her name happens to be Julia Morgan." After the building was completed, another woman reporter came to see it. Standing in the dining room, which was decorated with gold, gray, ivory, and scarlet, she said to Ms. Morgan, "How you must have reveled in this chance to squeeze dry the loveliest tubes in the whole world of color!" Ms. Morgan replied, "I don't think you understand just what my work here has been. The decorative part was done by a New York firm. My work has all been structural."[20]

• Famed architect Frank Lloyd Wright designed architecture as works of art, but he also was capable of being very practical. He invented toilets that hung from the wall and stall partitions that hung from the ceiling to make mopping easier. In addition, when he designed the Imperial Hotel in Tokyo, Japan, he was aware of the risk of earthquakes and fires resulting from them, so he designed a courtyard pool to serve both as an aesthetic element and as a source of water to fight fires following an earthquake that cut off the usual water supply. Shortly after it was completed, the Imperial Hotel survived with little damage a devastating earthquake, and the courtyard pool provided water to fight the fires that sprang up after the earthquake.[21]

• Thomas Jefferson designed his home, Monticello. Looked at from the outside, Monticello appeared to have one story (with a domed room above), but that is an illusion consciously created by Mr. Jefferson. On the second story, the windows are close to the floor, while on the first story the windows are close to the ceiling. Looked at from the outside, the windows appear to be providing light to one story. Mr. Jefferson based this design on windows he had admired while in France.[22]

• Architect Frank Lloyd Wright once created a house for a cousin named Richard Lloyd Jones. Unfortunately, after the house was built, the roof leaked when it rained. Mr. Jones' wife, Georgia, joked, "That's what happens when you leave a work of art out in the rain."[23]

Art

• In 1955, Marcia Brown's book *Cinderella* won the Caldecott Medal. Charles Scribner's Sons published it, although Viking Press might have published it if it weren't for a strike by elevator operators in the 1940s. After Ms. Brown had completed her first picture-book, *The Little Carousel*, she decided to take it to various publishers to see if they wanted it. Her first choice was Viking Press, but their offices were on the seventh floor, and she didn't want to climb that many steps. Since the offices of Charles Scribner's Sons were on the fourth floor, she stopped there first. They were interested in *The Little Carousel*, they published it, and they continued to publish books by her.[24]

• When Alison Bechdel, creator of *Dykes to Watch Out For*, first created the character of Mo, she based the character on herself — "a young, white, middle-class, marginally employed lesbian-feminist." However, she attempted to disguise this fact by drawing Mo with glasses and with hair longer than her own. The attempt was unsuccessful — her friends easily see her in the character and laugh when she tells them about the disguise.[25]

Caricatures

• One of the ways that comedian Whoopi Goldberg knew that she was beginning to make it big was that caricaturist Harry Hirschfeld worked his art on her in *The New York Times* while she was appearing on a one-woman show on Broadway. Mr. Hirschfeld traditionally hides his daughter's name — Nina — in his caricatures, and in his caricature of Ms. Goldberg he wrote "Nina" 40 times. Ms. Goldberg was so pleased with Mr. Hirschfeld's caricature that she sent him flowers.[26]

• Enrico Caruso was a caricaturist as well as a gifted opera singer. In addition, Mr. Caruso was a genuinely likeable human being. The composer Victor Herbert was a big man, and he said of Mr. Caruso,

"Even in his caricatures he shows the sweetness of his nature. He has never drawn me as fat as others have."[27]

• Zero Mostel was funny both on- and offstage. When caricaturist Sam Norkin arrived at a rehearsal to sketch Mr. Mostel and co-star Eli Wallach for an illustration of Eugène Ionesco's *Rhinoceros*, Mr. Mostel took him aside and said, "Here's $20. Leave Eli out of the drawing."[28]

Cartoons

• Jennifer Camper's cartoon *subGURLZ* features three lesbians: 1) Swizzle, who is the strongest woman on Earth. She works in a bar, and when sexually harassed by men, attempts to push them away without hurting them, but tends to accidentally break their necks. 2) Liver, who is on a constant diet of alcohol, tobacco, legal and illegal drugs, and even drain-unplugging products in an attempt to balance the chemicals in her body. She also has the power to bring the recently deceased back to life. 3) Byte, who is so intelligent that hair doesn't grow on her head. Her hobby is breaking into computer databases and moving funds from the accounts of greedy corporations to the accounts of people who need the money to do such things as go to college. If you ask Ms. Camper whether these subGURLZ are good or evil, she replies, "It depends. Whose side are you on?"[29]

• Garry Trudeau first started publishing a cartoon titled *Bull Tales* in the *Yale Record*, a magazine at Yale University. He then showed samples of the cartoon to Reed Hundt, editor of the *Yale Daily News*, the campus newspaper. Mr. Hundt looked over the sample cartoons and then said, "They're all right. We publish pretty much anything." Later, *Bull Tales* became better known as *Doonesbury*.[30]

Censorship

• Marty Links drew the comic strip *Emmy Lou* for 34 years, but she ended it in 1979 because her syndicate would not allow her to have her characters discuss controversies such as the Vietnam War, which her own three children — who were teenagers like Emmy Lou — were discussing. In 1970, she wanted to introduce a black character, but her syndicate forbade her to because Southern newspapers would not run the strip.[31]

• At the beginning of the 20th century, political cartoonists made fun of a governor of Pennsylvania by drawing his likeness in the form of a fat parrot, so the governor helped pass a law that made it illegal for artists to depict human beings as birds or animals. The cartoonists responded by drawing the governor's likeness in the form of a fat vegetable.[32]

• A visitor to the studio of painter James McNeill Whistler saw a nude painting hanging on the wall and asked, "Isn't that indecent?" Mr. Whistler replied, "No, madam, but your question is."[33]

Children

• As a child, American realist painter Andrew Wyeth was a little rascal. One day, while riding in the back seat of the family car, Andrew threw some firecrackers — which he had lit — under the front seat. He also once hid behind a curtain near the christening font in church. While the minister gave his sermon, Andrew made faces at the congregation. In addition, he once wanted to shoplift a candy bar, so he tried to make a little girl be his lookout. She didn't want to do it, so he put the candy bar in one of her pockets and then laughed as he ran away. Perhaps not surprisingly, young Andrew's hands were never still. When his father, the eminent illustrator N.C. Wyeth, tried to paint young Andrew's portrait in *Andy with Fire Engine*, he was forced to leave the hands unfinished.[34]

• Bill Peet has written and illustrated many picture-books for children, such as *Big Bad Bruce* and *Hubert's Hair-Raising Adventure*, but for a while he wanted to create high-brow paintings. After working at Disney for years, he started a painting, but he was disappointed with the results. The painting seemed to him to be "dull and uninspired," and soon he lost interest in it. However, Billy, his very young son, liked to paint, and while his father was away, Billy worked on the painting. At first, Mr. Peet's wife, Margaret, was worried that he would be angry, but in fact he was relieved that he didn't have to finish the painting. Soon afterward, he discovered his true calling and started to create the children's picture-books for which he became famous.[35]

• As a child, Jerry Butler used a stick to draw in the red dirt in his yard in Magnolia, Mississippi. Often his drawings went unnoticed, but when he drew a picture of his relatives, his grandmother Artise (whom he called Grand Mo Lu) called for everyone to come and look at what he had created. Afterward, whenever someone would ask the kids in the family what they wanted to be when they grew up and young Jerry would answer that he wanted to be an FBI agent or something like that, Grand Mo Lu would tell him, "You're already an artist. That's enough to be." When he grew up, Mr. Butler did become a professional artist — and a writer, too — and he created such books as *A Drawing in the Sand: A Story of African American Art*.[36]

• When Stan Berenstain, co-creator with Jan, his wife, of the Berenstain Bears books, was a small child, he went into a room that had been newly wallpapered. Even at his young age, he knew that he enjoyed drawing, and facing a wall in desperate need of decorating and armed with a red crayon in his hand, he went to work. Unfortunately, the adults in the house were not appreciative of his decorating efforts, and since it was a time that not only allowed but also encouraged spanking, he ended up suffering for his art.[37]

• After publishing his children's book *And to Think That I Saw It on Mulberry Street*, Dr. Seuss presented a program for 300 third-graders at Higbee's Department Store in Cleveland, Ohio. As part of the presentation, he drew several pictures. Unfortunately, the children did not respond to the drawings. Dr. Seuss asked, "Don't you like my drawing?" The children honestly replied, "No — Gus can draw better." Dr. Seuss invited Gus onto the stage to draw a picture — and yes, Gus did draw better than Dr. Seuss.[38]

• Ezra Jack Keats once created a children's picture-book titled *Pet Show!* about a child who took a germ to enter in a pet show. Tori Bond of Shaker Heights, Ohio, read the book, and she decided to enter a pet show in which no cats or dogs were allowed. (Her "real" pet was a cat.) Therefore, she coughed in a jar and named her pet germ Ralph. In a letter to Mr. Keats, she wrote, "I won first prize for most unusual pet. A doctor told me that Ralph eats cells."[39]

• Navaho artist R.C. "Rudy" Gorman was born prematurely. Because he was small and weak, his physician put him in an incubator to keep him warm and help him grow stronger. However, when his great-grandmother, a full-blooded Navajo, saw him in the incubator, she screamed, "Those crazy white people are killing your child!" She took Rudy away, fed him milk mixed with coffee, and soon the future artist grew big and strong without the incubator.[40]

• When photographer Margaret Bourke-White was a little girl, she decided to attract some attention at her school, so she wrapped two pet snakes around her arms and took the snakes to school. The snakes created quite a sensation, especially a harmless puff adder that puffed out its neck and hissed at the children. Young Margaret had fun, but the principal told her not to bring snakes to school anymore.[41]

• German artist Käthe Kollwitz once drew a portrait of herself and Peter, her seven-year-old son. The pose necessitated that she hold her son while drawing with one hand for long periods of time. This sometimes made her groan, but Peter would tell her, "Don't worry, Mother. It will be beautiful." Peter died in World War I, and Ms. Kollwitz created in his honor two statues titled *The Grieving Parents*.[42]

• Renaissance painter Giotto di Bondone created beautiful works of art, but he was ugly, and his children were ugly. When Dante, author of *The Divine Comedy*, asked about this paradox, Giotto replied that his children were produced in the dark of night while his works of art were created in the light of day.[43]

• One of American Impressionist Mary Cassatt's young nephews grew tired of posing for her, so he spat in her face. The boy's mother punished him by locking him in a closet, but Ms. Cassatt bought him some chocolates.[44]

• Trevor Mark Sage-EL has a white mother and a black father. He is very creative, and when his teacher asked him to draw a self-portrait at school, he drew a yin-yang symbol, which is half-black and half-white.[45]

Christmas

• Political cartoonist Thomas Nast was also famous for his drawings of Christmas and of Santa Claus, and he was responsible for many of the ideas we associate with Santa Claus — the red and white suit of clothing, the workshop at the North Pole, and the reading by Santa Claus of letters sent to him by children. In a drawing titled *Christmas Flirtation*, Mr. Nast drew Julia, his daughter, standing under some mistletoe. In England, boys followed the custom of kissing a girl and then removing a berry from the mistletoe. Once the berries were gone, the boys no longer were allowed to kiss the girl. The mistletoe that Julia is standing underneath is heavily laden with berries.[46]

• In the comic strip *Peanuts*, Lucy sometimes dispensed psychiatric help in a booth for 5 cents. One winter Benjamin Weininger, a psychiatrist at the Southern California Counseling Center in Los Angeles, followed her example. He sat in a lemonade stand bearing the sign, "In the Xmas Spirit ... Counseling 5 cents." However, Charles Schultz, the creator of *Peanuts*, pointed out that the sign was not entirely correct — when it's cold, Lucy raises her price to 7 cents.[47]

Clothing

• Early in her career, photographer Margaret Bourke-White had little money to spend on clothing. Her professional clothing consisted of one grey suit, with red accessories and blue accessories. She alternated the use of the red accessories and the blue accessories, and she kept notes of what she was wearing when she met with customers. If she had worn the red accessories the last time she had met a particular customer, she made sure to wear the blue accessories the next time she met that particular customer.[48]

• Gertrude Stein was able to buy paintings by Picasso and other famous artists early in their careers partly because she economized on clothing. In a conversation with Ernest Hemingway and his first wife, Hadley, she advised Hadley to buy clothes for durability and not for style, and to buy paintings with the money thus saved. During the conversation, Hadley had a difficult time refraining from looking at Ms. Stein's eccentric and decidedly unfashionable clothing.[49]

• Mexican artist Diego Rivera knew what was important in life. While he was living in Paris, a fire broke out in his apartment one night as he was sleeping. Mr. Rivera ran around, gathering paintings and taking them outside to safety. Only after he had saved several paintings did he discover that he wasn't wearing any pants.[50]

Chapter 2: From Collectors to Fathers

Collectors

• A man who had become rich through cheating the customers who shopped at his chain of stores spent millions to acquire works of art that he hung on his walls and gloated over. He often invited people to his mansion and asked them to point out anything that was not refined, but no one ever did. One day, the rich man invited a Buddhist monk to view his art collection. The monk said, "Your art collection is really exquisite and refined, but one thing is not in harmony with it." Surprised, the rich man asked, "What is that?" The monk replied, "You."[51]

• An Australian artist knew that soprano Frances Alda collected art, so he booked passage on a ship he knew she was sailing on, and he set up an exhibition in the ship's lounge. The captain of the ship invited her to the art exhibition, but unfortunately for the artist Ms. Alda was knowledgeable about art. She entered the ship's lounge, glanced at the paintings on display — then uttered "Good God!" and walked out.[52]

• A rich American wanted to buy a Rembrandt, but he owned no other paintings. Lord Duveen refused to sell it to him, saying, "I can't possibly sell a Rembrandt to a man who owns no other pictures. The Rembrandt would be lonely."[53]

• Even after Impressionist painter Edgar Degas' eyesight grew bad in his old age, he still collected works of art. One day he bought a painting at an auction and then asked a friend, "Is it beautiful?"[54]

Comics

• Did you know that the comic book heroine Wonder Woman was created for the purpose of serving as feminist propaganda? It's true. William Moulton Marston — the man who invented the technological basis of the lie detector — created Wonder Woman in the 1940s. He explained, "Wonder Woman is psychological propaganda for the new type of woman who should, I believe, rule the world. There isn't love enough in the male organism to rule this planet peacefully. ... I have given Wonder Woman this dominant force but have kept her loving, tender, maternal, and feminine in every other way." In other words, according to her creator, the purpose of Wonder Woman is to help brainwash young male comic book readers into allowing women to rule them.[55]

• Al Capp for many years wrote and drew the comic strip *Li'l Abner*. At a cocktail party, his hostess introduced him to a VIP. She said, "Mr. President, I'd like you to meet the famous comic strip cartoonist Al Capp." The President asked, "What comic strip?" After answering the President's question, the hostess then said, "Mr. Capp, I'd like to introduce the President." Mr. Capp asked, "What country?"[56]

• One of the things that Stan Lee did to make Marvel comic books interesting to the reader was to write entertaining credits for the stories. For example, "Written with Passion by Stan Lee. Drawn with Pride by Jack Kirby. Inked with Perfection by Joe Sinnott. And Lettered with a Scratchy Pen by Artie Simek."[57]

Costumes

• When George Balanchine's *Four Temperaments* was premiered at Ballet Society's premier performance (a doubly historic event), everything was a smash success — except for the costumes, which had been designed by artist Kurt Seligmann, who neglected to design costumes that did not obscure the dancing. Mr. Balanchine was aware of the problem, and after the premiere, he asked Mr. Seligmann, "Can't we modify and cut away fabric? Costumes are blocking choreography. No one can see steps." Unfortunately, Mr. Seligmann objected, "If we cut fabric and change costumes, yes, we will see choreography, but then no one will see the designs. No one will see Seligmann!" For a while, at least, the costumes stayed.[58]

• When artist Marc Chagall designed the costumes for ballerina Alicia Markova's performance in Léonide Massine's *Aleko*, he occasionally sent notes to Ms. Markova. He once drew a heart and signed his name inside it — and then he told Ms. Markova that he was sending his heart to her.[59]

Crime

• On 22 April 1911, the security guards of the Louvre Museum were busy, and someone stole the *Mona Lisa* by simply walking out the door with it under his arm wrapped in a workman's smock. For two years, it was missing, until finally the thief contacted Alfredo Geri, a Florentine art dealer. Mr. Geri in turn contacted the police, and they recovered the famous painting, which had been stolen by a house painter named Vincenzo Peruggia. He had worked at the Louvre, and he had stolen the *Mona Lisa* because he felt that its true home was in Italy. The *Mona Lisa* was returned to the Louvre, where it can be seen today.[60]

• American artist Keith Haring sold paintings and drawings for thousands of dollars, but he also used to create art for free in such locations as the New York City subways in order to attract a wide audience. Since Mr. Haring didn't want to be a vandal, he created his art on the black paper used to cover unused billboards. Nevertheless, creating art on the black paper was illegal, and on a few occasions, he was arrested by police officers who fingerprinted him and then asked for his autograph.[61]

• Oscar Wilde had a low regard for USAmericans' knowledge of art. He told a story about a former Rocky Mountain miner ordering a plaster reproduction of the Venus de Milo and being shocked that when it arrived, it had no arms. He sued the company that had sold it to him — and a USAmerican court awarded him damages![62]

• When Valerie Solanis shot Andy Warhol, he collapsed onto the floor, bleeding profusely. Factory regular Billy Name got to him first, and Mr. Warhol told him, "Don't ... don't ... don't make me laugh. It hurts too much."[63]

• Pablo Picasso once arrived home to find that he was the victim of a burglary. However, none of his paintings were stolen, only some table linen and his bed.[64]

Critics

• After art critics panned the work of Sarah Bixby Smith, the wife of author Paul Jordan-Smith, he was angry, and he decided to paint a work of art in a style that he thought the critics would like. Therefore, he created a crude painting of a woman holding a banana, and he showed it to his wife. They had a good laugh, then forgot about the painting until one of their sons brought home as his guest the art critic of the local newspaper. The art critic loved the painting and asked for information about the artist. Being a creative person, Mr. Jordan-Smith made up on the spot a name — Pavel Jerdanowitch, a foreign-sounding version of his first two names — and a school of art that he called Disumbrationism. Amazed by the reaction of the local art critic, Mr. Jordan-Smith then entered the painting in a major art exhibit in 1925. A Paris art magazine published a long article about the painting, and its editor wrote Mr. Jerdanowitch for information about his life. Mr. Jordan-Smith happily responded to the letter with made-up information. The following year, Mr. Jordan-Smith created another painting — portraying a large woman washing clothes — and exhibited it in Chicago. This time, *Art World* magazine published a story about the exhibition and printed a photograph of the painting in its article. Mr. Jordan-Smith kept the hoax going for a while longer before revealing it. Even that didn't stop interest in Mr. Jerdanowitch. In 1927, the Vose Galleries of Boston exhibited four "Jerdanowitch" paintings so that the public could see what had fooled the experts.[65]

• Nineteenth-century cartoonist Bernhard Gillam's first attempt at oil painting was a dismal failure. When he was eighteen years old, he painted a battle between the Aztec Native Americans and the Spanish explorers. The painting was filled with dead and dying soldiers, but when exhibited at the Brooklyn Academy of Fine Arts as number 93, it did not produce the seriously dramatic effect Mr. Gillam wanted. A reviewer in the Brooklyn *Eagle* wrote, "The sensation of the hour is number 93. There was never anything funnier than the dying men in 93, unless it is the men who are already dead. Don't fail to see it; it's the greatest show on earth!" Mr. Gillam used to stand near his painting, listening to people laugh at what he had meant to be a deadly serious painting.[66]

• Movie director Billy Wilder was friends with chef Wolfgang Puck, and whenever Mr. Wilder went to Mr. Puck's restaurant, the two usually spoke German together. One day, as the two were talking, actor Tony Curtis came in with some of his paintings to hang in an exhibition at the restaurant. Mr. Wilder knew art, and his own collection included works by Picasso and Matisse. He looked at a few of Mr. Curtis' paintings and then said to Mr. Puck, "Lousy actor; lousy painter." Mr. Curtis looked shocked, and Mr. Wilder immediately apologized: "I'm sorry. I thought I was speaking German."[67]

• The painter Chien-to brought a painting for Emperor Sun-si, Prince Wej, and the Buddhist priest Si-tien to examine. Both Emperor Sun-si and Prince Wej praised the painting's complete harmony, but then Chien-to picked up a piece of mud and threw it onto a corner of the painting. Emperor Sun-si asked Chien-to, "Why did you spoil the complete harmony of your painting?" However, Si-tien spoke up: "He has made the painting true to life, for always in life, when everything seems completely in harmony, there is somewhere hidden, not easily visible, a piece of mud."[68]

• Many art critics respected the primitive art of Grandma Moses, but others did not. One critic remarked, "A primitive is an artist who doesn't know much about painting but knows what people like." Other people thought that the popularity of Grandma Moses' art was merely a passing fad. When gallery director Otto Kallir wrote her a letter intended to comfort her because of the critical attacks on herself and her art, Grandma Moses wrote back, "This is a free country, and people will talk. Let them; if we do what is right, they can't hurt us."[69]

• In the late 1950s, Robert Hughes wrote an occasional book review and created cartoons for the Australian newspaper *Observer*. One day, the editor announced, "I've just fired the art critic. Anyone here know anything about art?" He looked at Mr. Hughes and said, "You're the cartoonist. You ought to know something about art. Good. Well, now you're the f**king art critic." Good choice. Mr. Hughes became a renowned critic.[70]

• After *Punch* published a parody of a conversation between Oscar Wilde and James McNeill Whistler, Mr. Wilde sent Mr. Whistler this telegram: "*Punch* too ridiculous. When you and I are together, we never talk about anything except ourselves." Mr. Whistler replied by telegram, "No, no, Oscar, you forget. When you and I are together, we never talk about anything except me."[71]

• James McNeill Whistler wasn't afraid to use his devastating wit — even against the people who paid him to paint their portrait. One male patron complained, "Do you consider that a great work of art?" Mr. Whistler replied, "Do you consider yourself a great work of nature?"[72]

• Not all great paintings are liked. After Paul Gauguin finished painting a portrait of Marie-Angélique Satre, wife of the mayor of Pont-Aven, she looked at it (its title is *La Belle Angèle*), called it a "horror," and would not keep it in her home.[73]

• On a flight, Alfred E. Kahn showed Soviet ballerina Galina Ulanova a copy of *Wilson's Dictionary of Ballet*. She looked at the drawings of basic ballet positions and then shook her head and used a pencil to correct them.[74]

Death

• In the early 20th century, a French landscape painter named Andre Marcellin decided to branch out into portraits. He painted the portrait of a banker, and a few days after the painting was finished, the banker died. He painted the portrait of a woman, and a few days after the painting was finished, the woman died. He painted the portrait of a friend, and a few days after the painting was finished, the friend died. After that, he declined to paint any more portraits for five years. Then he met a woman and became engaged to her. She insisted that he paint her portrait, even though he explained that his portraits were cursed. Eventually he gave in because she told him that she would not marry him unless he painted her portrait. A few days after the painting was finished, she died. Soon afterward, Mr. Marcellin painted his last portrait: a portrait of himself. A few days after the painting was finished, he died.[75]

• In 1955, when she was 95 years old, artist Grandma Moses was interviewed by journalist Edward R. Murrow for his television show *See It Now*. During the show, Mr. Morrow asked, "What are you going to do for the next 20 years, Grandma Moses?" In reply, she pointed upward and said, "I am going up yonder. Naturally, naturally I should. After you get to be about so old, you can't expect to go on much further." Grandma Moses died at age 101. (Mr. Murrow had wanted to do the interview in Grandma Moses' bedroom, where she did her painting, but she didn't think any man other than a husband had any business in a lady's bedroom, so she moved her painting supplies to the living room, where the interview took place.)[76]

• Léon Bakst, a Russian painter and set designer for Sergei Diaghilev's ballets, once fell in love with a beautiful young Frenchwoman in Paris. He took her to Versailles because he hoped that such a romantic location might make her romantic. They sat down together, Mr. Bakst moved closer to her, and she remarked to him, "What a wonderful place for a suicide."[77]

• In Highgate Cemetery in London, many tourists visit the grave of Elizabeth Eleanor Siddal, who was the wife and model of the painter Dante Gabriel Rossetti. When she died in 1862, Mr. Rossetti buried some poems with her. However, in 1869, he reconsidered and had her grave dug up so he could retrieve the poems.[78]

Education

• East German gymnast Erika Zuchold quickly discovered another career after leaving gymnastics following the 1972 Olympic Games in Munich, where she won silver medals on both vault and uneven bars. As a gymnast, she often drew pictures before and during competitions to reduce her nervousness. In addition, after she tore her Achilles tendon and could not compete in the 1964 Olympic Games in Tokyo, she drew as a means of coping with her disappointment. Fans had sent flowers to her hospital room, and so she drew flowers. Each time she drew the flowers, her drawing became more skilled. After retiring from gymnastics, she studied art education at Karl Marx University in Leipzig. She taught art, and she had art exhibitions in Germany, Iraq, Spain, and Switzerland.[79]

• Jackson Pollock was an American rebel at a young age. While attending Manual Arts High School in Los Angeles, he distributed an underground newspaper that criticized the values of the school, suggesting that academics should be valued more than football. One sentence of the newspaper stated, "Instead of 'hit that line,' we should cry 'make that grade.'" After being caught twice distributing the underground newspaper, young Jackson was expelled for the rest of the school year. When he returned to school, he was wearing long hair. In pursuit of conformity, some members of the football team forcibly cut his hair.[80]

• Leonardo da Vinci was a problem-solver in addition to being an artist. In his studies of human anatomy, he dissected human cadavers or parts of human cadavers, although embalming had not been invented yet. In doing this, he had to figure out how to dissect a human eyeball. After all, the inside of an eye is filled with a liquid jelly. Eventually, he discovered that he could harden the eyeball for dissection by coating it with egg white and then boiling it. Leonardo noted that this work was not pleasant — "passing the night hours in the company of these corpses, quartered and flayed and horrible to behold."[81]

• Canadian figure skater Toller Cranston attended the École des Beaux-Arts, where he showed great talent as a painter, but failed a class in sculpture. He told his sculpture teacher, Joan Essar, "Look, I'm not really a sculptor. It's not my thing. As a matter of fact, I'm having a painting exhibition in Toronto." Ms. Essar and a couple of other art teachers looked at some of his paintings, which impressed them, and then they asked him, "What do you want to be? An art teacher or an artist?" He replied that he wanted to be an artist, and they advised him, "Don't bother finishing school." He didn't.[82]

• Early in his life, Marc Chagall attended Russia's Svantseva School, where his art teacher was Léon Bakst. Mr. Bakst could be a harsh critic of students' work, and after being harshly criticized, Mr. Chagall left the school for three months to study on his own. When he returned, he had made much progress. Mr. Bakst praised his art and even hung one of his paintings in the studio. About his famous pupil, Mr. Bakst said, "What I like about him is that after listening closely to my lessons he takes his paints and brushes and does something absolutely different from what I have told him."[83]

• When touring Florence in 1952, George Balanchine's dance troupe was in theory supposed to use their energy for dancing, but George Balanchine did not object when many dancers spent much energy touring museums and looking at the works of art. Much earlier, Sergei Diaghilev had encouraged the young George Balanchine to often tour art museums and keep looking at works of art that at first were alien to him. One day, Mr. Balanchine experienced a revelation while looking at the works of art: "One day I saw them. I could really *see* them. I knew why he made me go back."[84]

• Stan and Jan Berenstain are the creators of the Berenstain Bears. As you would expect, they both liked to draw from an early age. When Jan was a little girl in elementary school, she broke her collarbone play-wrestling with another girl. The doctor put her arm in a sling and told her not to use that arm for a while. Because Jan liked drawing, when it came time for art class, she tried to take her arm out of the sling so she could draw, but her teacher made put her arm back in the sling. Jan read a book while everyone else drew.[85]

• Famed architect Frank Lloyd Wright had a vision of creating a distinctly American architecture early in his career. Because Mr. Wright showed promise as a young architect, two men, architect David Burnham and a wealthy man named Ed Waller, offered to send him to Paris to study for four years at the Beaux-Arts — all expenses paid — provided he returned to the United States and designed houses in the European classical style. Mr. Wright turned down the offer.[86]

• At the University of Washington in Seattle, Jacob Lawrence was an excellent teacher in addition to being a world-class (and African-American) artist. One day, an art student brought a bad painting for Mr. Lawrence to look at and told him that the painting was exactly the kind he wished to paint — it was painted in his "style." Mr. Lawrence looked at the painting and then told the student, "Don't bluff. If you paint, do it well or not at all."[87]

• When James McNeill Whistler was at West Point, he took a drawing class with Robert W. Weir. In one class, Mr. Whistler drew a young girl. Mr. Weir picked up a pencil and was about to make corrections to the drawing, but Mr. Whistler cried, "Don't, sir, don't! You'll spoil it!" Mr. Weir understood Mr. Whistler's feelings and did not correct the drawing.[88]

• Children's book author/illustrator Vera B. Williams had fun with children when she gave presentations in school. Sometimes, she drew an oval on a chalkboard and asked the children if it is a boy or a girl. Some children answered, "A boy," while others answered, "A girl," and then Ms. Williams told them, "Don't be silly. It's a potato."[89]

• People who read the satiric magazine *MAD* picked up useful information. A Danish fan of *MAD* once visited New York City. He was able to identify the strange insects in his hotel room because in *MAD* he had read about and seen illustrations of cockroaches.[90]

• Choreographer Léonide Massine once saw Pablo Picasso carefully study a painting that was conventional, so he asked him why he was studying that particular painting. Mr. Picasso replied, "I am studying it carefully in order to learn how not to paint."[91]

Exhibitions

• Hugh Troy once attended a crowded exhibition of paintings by Vincent Van Gogh, but he felt that the numerous viewers at the museum were more interested in the lurid details of the painter's life — such as cutting off his ear so he could give it to a prostitute — than in the paintings themselves. Therefore, Mr. Troy used his talents as an artist to fashion a severed ear (using dried beef) and to construct a box with the inscription "This is the ear that Van Gogh cut off and sent to his mistress Dec. 24, 1888." Placing the ear in the box, Mr. Troy smuggled it into the museum and then unobtrusively placed it in the exhibit. Almost immediately, everyone crowded around the "ear" and ignored the paintings. This allowed Mr. Troy to get close to the paintings and enjoy them.[92]

• As a radical who broke new ground in art, Mary Cassatt rejected some things that many artists accept. After she was informed that she had won a $300 Walter Lippincott Prize for work shown in the 1904 exhibition at the Pennsylvania Academy of Fine Arts, she turned down the prize, writing, "Of course it is very gratifying to know that a picture of mine was selected for a special honor. I, however, who belong to the founders of the Independent Exhibition, must stick to my principles, our principles, which were, no jury, no medals, no awards."[93]

• One of artist Louise Nevelson's early exhibitions was of a group of sculptures she titled *Circus*. The exhibition received rave critical reviews, but none of the works of art she had exhibited sold. Ms. Nevelson was so angry that she dismantled the sculptures and burned them. She also burned approximately 200 of her paintings. Because of this explosion of anger, very few of her works of art from before 1943 exist today.[94]

• By the 1970s, African-American folk artist Clementine Hunter had become famous, although she had not started to paint until she was 53 years old. President Jimmy Carter sent her an invitation to attend an exhibition of her work in Washington, D.C., but Ms. Hunter had been born in 1886 and she did not like to travel. She said, "If Jimmy Carter wants to see me, he knows where I am. He can come here."[95]

• American Impressionist artist Mary Cassatt was talking with some friends at an Impressionist exhibition in Paris when a woman turned to her and said, "But you are forgetting a foreign painter who [Edgar] Degas thinks is first rate." Ms. Cassatt asked, "Who is that?" The woman replied, "Mary Cassatt." Ms. Cassatt said, "Oh, nonsense," and the woman turned away, murmuring, "She's jealous."[96]

• Berenice Abbott once exhibited her photographs in Brussels, but although they sold well, she didn't receive any money from them. The art dealer who had arranged the exhibition kept the money, telling her that he "did not have the courage to be poor."[97]

Fathers

• Stanislaus Szulkalski was a Polish sculptor who always met his father for a walk every Sunday morning in a park in Chicago. One day, he arrived at the park to find a crowd around his father, who had died after being run over by a car. At the hospital, people asked what he wanted to do with the body. Mr. Szulkalski was poor, and he didn't have the money to bury his father. In addition, he was an artist who was too poor to pay for lessons to learn about human anatomy. So he solved two problems at the same time — he took his father's body home and dissected it, thus disposing of the body and learning about human anatomy. Later, people looked at his sculpture and told him that he certainly knew a lot about human anatomy — they also asked how he had come by that knowledge. Mr. Szulkalski always answered, "My father taught me."[98]

• The father of American realist painter Andrew Wyeth was the eminent illustrator N.C. Wyeth, who trained his son to be able to follow his profession. As a young man, Andrew was given a book to illustrate, but he struggled with the assignment because the book was so badly written. His father knew why he was struggling, so he told him, "Andy, it's utterly ridiculous for you to do that book. Go to Maine and paint like hell! I will support you. You don't have to be an illustrator." Andrew followed his father's advice, winning his father's praise for the work he did. In fact, Andrew succeeded so well that soon a young painter asked N.C., "By God, are you the father of Andrew Wyeth?" N.C., of course, was disgusted by this question, preferring to be known for his own work.[99]

• The father of choreographer Bella Lewitzky taught her the importance of having an art to practice. He worked an ordinary job, but when he came home, he painted. Ms. Lewitzky says, "He taught me that it didn't make a d*mn bit of difference what you did for a living, as long as you had something that rewarded your life." He also didn't feel that it was necessary to have an audience for his art because the act of creation was rewarding in itself. Bella and her sister used to steal their father's paintings — because if they didn't, he would paint another work of art on top of the one he had already created.[100]

Chapter 3: From Food to Museums

Food

• Tom Clark of Davidson, North Carolina, is famous for his designs of gnomes. He has designed well over 1,000 gnomes, and in 2006 he estimated that a complete collection would cost a collector approximately $200,000. His fans are around the world, and one fan who brought Mr. Clark to his house to autograph all his gnomes took him as his guest behind the scenes of a movie starring Lloyd Bridges. They ate lunch with the cast of the movie, and the gnome collector showed members of the cast a catalog filled with Clark's gnomes. A woman at lunch, who also collected Clark's gnomes, asked if the gnomes were by Mr. Clark, and the gnome collector replied, "Yes," then he pointed to Mr. Clark and added, "And that's Tom Clark." The shocked woman choked on her food and had to be rescued with the Heimlich maneuver.[101]

• In the late 19th century, preachers in the United States were sometimes paid in part in the form of food. When architect Frank Lloyd Wright was eight years old in 1875, dinner in the household of his preacher father sometimes consisted of seven varieties of pie.[102]

Forgeries

• The Metropolitan Museum of Art in New York City collected three magnificent examples of Etruscan sculpture in the early 20th century: two full-sized fierce warriors and a helmeted head that was over five feet tall. Many experts thought that the sculptures were genuine, but a few argued that they were fakes. In 1960, art expert Harold Parsons proved that they were fakes by finding the man who had created them. Alfredo Fioravanti and his partners had worked in the business of restoring antiquities before they started to create their own. They created pieces that were so large that they couldn't be fired whole, so they broke them in pieces and then fired them. After creating the pieces, they gave them to an art dealer who then sold them to the Metropolitan Museum of Art. After Mr. Parsons revealed that the statues were fakes, they were re-examined, and scholars discovered that the "Greek black" glaze of the statues contained the dye magnesium dioxide, which was not available to the Etruscans. Of course, that was enough to prove that the statues were fakes, but Mr. Fioravanti had another convincing piece of evidence. When he had created one of the stone warriors, a thumb had broken off. Mr. Fioravanti had kept the thumb, and when he held it against the statue, the fit was perfect.[103]

• Husband-and-wife children's book author/illustrator team Martin and Alice Provensen created such picture-books as the Caldecott Medal-winning *The Glorious Flight: Across the Channel with Louis Blériot.* This book is about the first man to fly solo across the English Channel, a feat he accomplished in 1909. One of their copies of the book has an inscription written in French. Translated, it says, "For the Provensens — Alice and Martin — with my sincere good wishes, Louis Blériot." No, the famous French aviator, who died in 1936, did not write the inscription — Mr. Provensen forged it. Inscriptions are not the only things he forged. Before his death in 1987, he frequently forged masterworks by such artists as Picasso and Rembrandt. He hung the forgeries in his and his wife's home, and he enjoyed watching the faces of their visitors as they tried to figure out how the Provensens could afford to own such masterpieces.[104]

Gays and Lesbians

• Alison Bechdel is a lesbian who draws the comic strip *Dykes to Look Out For.* Her comic strip started out as little drawings of lesbians she created in the margins of letters to friends. She began numbering the drawings — for example, "Dykes to Watch Out For, No. 75" — even though at that point she had drawn only three or four. Because her friends liked the drawings, she submitted them to a feminist newspaper titled *Womanews.* The drawings were accepted, and her comic strip developed from those early drawings.[105]

• Author Michael Thomas Ford, most notable for his books on LGBT activism and Pride and his "My Queer Life" series of comedic essay collections, is far from being fashion conscious and has a difficult time being presentable at fashionable events. For a photo shoot, Mr. Ford was asked to bring along some clothes to be photographed in. The photographer looked over the shirts that Mr. Ford had brought, and then he took off his own shirt, handed it to Mr. Ford, and said, "Put this on." The photographer remained shirtless for the duration of the shoot.[106]

Gifts

• When King Charles II visited St. John's College, Oxford, he was much taken with a portrait of Charles I and asked that the Head of the College give it to him. The Head of the College was unwilling to do so, so the King said, "I will grant you any favor in return." With this proviso, the Head of the College gave him the portrait. "Thank you," King Charles II said. "What now is your request?" The Head of the College replied, "Give it back." (The portrait can still be seen at the College.)[107]

• Bruno, the pet dog of children's book illustrator Victoria Chess, frequently brings to her odd presents — a dead squirrel, a dead woodchuck, a live chicken, a red ball with blue stars, a bottle of suntan lotion, etc. Ms. Chess jokes that the best present he ever brought to her was a purse belonging to a neighbor lady — not only did the purse contain $80, but it also contained 15 credit cards![108]

Inspiration

• Dr. Seuss got an idea for a book when a gust of wind blew a drawing of an elephant on top of a drawing of a tree. He looked at the two drawings and then asked himself, "An elephant in a tree — what's he doing there?" Then he answered his own question: "Of course! He's hatching an egg!" This idea resulted in Dr. Seuss' book *Horton Hatches an Egg*.[109]

• Bil Keane is the artist behind the comic strip *The Family Circle*. One day, while he was drawing the cartoon, his young son Jeffy watched him for a while and then asked, "Daddy, how do you know what to draw?" Mr. Keane replied, "God tells me." Jeffy asked next, "Then why do you keep erasing parts of it?"[110]

Landscapes

• John Banvard worked for years on a painting of the Mississippi River, eventually producing a work of art that was first displayed in Louisville, Kentucky, in 1845 — the painting was three miles long. To enable people to see it, it was exhibited like a scroll that was unrolled from one spindle onto another spindle. He exhibited the painting in the United States and England, but when he died it was cut up into pieces, some of which were used as backdrops for plays.[111]

• Winston Churchill was an amateur painter. Once he showed a group of landscapes to a friend, who asked why he painted only landscapes and not portraits. Sir Winston replied, "Because a tree doesn't complain that I haven't done it justice."[112]

Language

• In the 1970s, Ohio University President Claude Sowle decided to hold public meetings at which college deans would argue for money for their departments. Of course, these were spectacular events at which college deans wore caps and gowns and argued passionately for money. At one such public meeting, Dr. Henry Lin, Dean of Fine Arts, began his remarks by saying, "*Ni hao*, Dr. Sowle." Of course, he was speaking flawless Mandarin Chinese, and he continued to speak flawless Mandarin Chinese — which Dr. Sowle did NOT understand — for the rest of his remarks, occasionally using a Chinese abacus to emphasize a financial point. At the end of Dr. Lin's remarks, President Sowle told him, "Henry, you know I don't understand Chinese, but I've never understood you more clearly than right now — you need big bucks!" (By the way, the late Dr. Lin is the father of Maya Lin, who designed the Vietnam Veterans Memorial in Washington, D.C.)[113]

• As a child, Oliver W. Harrington, an African American, put out a six-page newspaper, written and drawn by hand, which was eagerly awaited each month by his South Bronx classmates. In one issue, young Oliver wrote about "Jewtown," a term that was commonly used to denote a part of the Bronx. One of his teachers, Mrs. Linsky, read the issue and then privately explained to him about the evil that lay behind such terms as "Jewtown" and "N*ggertown." He learned quickly and was hurt when he learned what he had done; after all, his mother was a Hungarian Jew. When he grew up, he became a famous political cartoonist who used his talents to fight for social justice.[114]

• Children's book illustrator Victoria Chess grew up speaking languages other than English. She didn't understand English until she was three years old, and she didn't let anyone know she could understand English until she was four. Why not? People say interesting things in English if they think you don't know that language.[115]

Lighting

• Light is very important in art museums. Lots of light can reveal details in a painting, but too much light can damage other works of art, so lighting is carefully controlled in art museums. Because too much light can damage light-sensitive art, sometimes employees of the National Gallery of Art in Washington, D.C., cover the skylights to keep light out of certain rooms. When Henri Matisse's wall-size paper cutouts were displayed, the room was not brightly lit because of the fragility of the paper he used. Also, they were lit for only half of the day. At 1 p.m. the lights went off and the doors to the exhibit closed. By the way, the National Gallery has glaziers — people who replace broken glass panes — on its payroll. After all, the National Gallery has many skylights, the glass panes of which are sometimes broken by stones dropped by seagulls. In addition, the National Gallery makes sure that lots of light is present where visitors enter the museum. It doesn't want visitors to trip and fall because they are blinded after coming into the museum from the brightly lit outdoors.[116]

• In the late 1800s and early 1900s, Jacob A. Riis became famous for his photographs of poor people in New York City tenements. His photographs showed *How the Other Half Lives* — the title of one of his books. In the early days of photography, getting enough light to photograph indoors could be a problem. He used to make a fire in a frying pan and use it to light his flash powder. If that didn't work well enough, he would shoot a revolver and use the light of its flash to take his photographs. Occasionally, Mr. Riis' lighting techniques started fires. He once caught his own clothes on fire, and he twice accidentally set fire to buildings. In addition, when a flash went off too close to his eyes, he almost blinded himself. However, his muckraking photographs, articles, and books led to social reforms to help poor people.[117]

• When Daniel Chester French's gigantic sculpture of Abraham Lincoln in the Lincoln Memorial was unveiled, the lighting was not satisfactory. Mr. French had designed the statue to be lit from above, but unfortunately the light illuminating the statue was coming from below, which gave Lincoln's face a surprised look. The statue was still cherished despite the poor lighting, and conditions for viewing it vastly improved in 1926 with the addition of artificial lighting to the ceiling of the Lincoln Memorial.[118]

Mishaps

• Mexican artist José Clemente Orozco created fresco paintings, working with watercolors on wet plaster so that the watercolors soaked into the plaster and created a permanent painting that was part of the wall. In 1932, he arrived at Dartmouth College in Hanover, New Hampshire, where he demonstrated fresco painting to students. The first day he was scheduled to paint a fresco on a wall whose surface had already been prepared by a mason, several students and professors showed up to watch him. Unfortunately, the surface would not take the watercolors — they simply dripped down the wall and were not absorbed into the plaster. Later, Mr. Orozco questioned the mason and discovered that he had used a special kind of plaster for the wall. The mason told him, "There can't be anything wrong with the plaster — it's guaranteed to be waterproof."[119]

• Al Capp, creator of the comic strip *Li'l Abner*, lost his leg after falling into the path of a trolley car when he was nine years old, and he was forced to use a wooden leg the rest of his life. He declined to take care of his leg, with the result that it sometimes deserted him when he needed it. One day, while he was walking with boxer Gene Tunney, he suddenly felt a need to grab onto something for balance, so he grabbed onto Mr. Tunney. Together, they looked back and saw the lower part of Mr. Capp's wooden leg. Mr. Capp gathered up the fallen leg, bolts, and nuts, and then he took his wooden leg to a garage, where the mechanic quickly fixed it. In this case, the mishap was a blessing, as Mr. Capp did not have to hear the boring speech that he and Mr. Tunney had planned to attend.[120]

• When he was a child, African-American painter Horace Pippin entered a contest in which he was asked to draw a funny face. He mailed his drawing to Chicago, and soon his prize arrived in the mail: six colored pencils, two brushes, and a box of paint. Immediately, he began creating works of art. He cut out six circles from muslin fabrics and used the pencils to create scenes from the Bible. Fortunately, an elderly lady bought all the works of art. Unfortunately, soon afterward the elderly lady washed all the circles of muslin fabric, not realizing that the colored-pencil drawings would wash away along with any dirt. The contest became the genesis of a lifetime making art. As an adult artist, Mr. Pippin said, "Pictures just come to my mind, and then I tell my heart to go ahead."[121]

• Early in her career, when she was still a student, artist Edna Hibel was enthusiastically working on a fresco, standing on a big block to reach high up on a wall. Unfortunately, she stepped too far back to view her work with the result that she fell to the floor. Ms. Hibel says, "That's one time my enthusiasm hit bottom!"[122]

Models

• Mary Cassatt occasionally ran into model trouble. Early in her career, she tried to paint her father, but he kept falling asleep while posing and ruined the pose. She also tried to paint the Cassatt family's maid, Mrs. Currey, who quit before the portrait was finished. Later, in Seville, Spain, her models grew tired because Ms. Cassatt spent so many hours painting them. Ms. Cassatt even wrote that one of her models asked her "if the people who pose for me live long." And in the latter part of her career, people criticized her models because they were not good looking. Ms. Cassatt once wrote a letter defending her models against this kind of criticism: "So you think my models are not worthy of their clothes? You find their types coarse. I know that is an American newspaper criticism. Everyone has their conception of beauty. I confess I love health and strength."[123]

• As a young man, comedian Zero Mostel attended City College of New York, where most students were Jewish and which was known as a proletarian Harvard. One course he took was "life drawing," which meant drawing and painting the nude model, a burlesque stripper named Honey Bee Keller. When she dropped her kimono, Mr. Mostel would emit a wolf whistle that startled the students but did not faze Ms. Keller, who was used to it in her line of work. While painting, Mr. Mostel continually made jokes, making other students laugh. Once, Mr. Mostel caused Honey Bee Keller to laugh so much that she fell off her stand and into the arms of a professor.[124]

• Artist Edgar Degas created realistic nudes of women, showing the imperfections of the individual's body rather than showing an idealized form. Asked why some of the nude women in his paintings were so ugly, Mr. Degas replied that women — in general — are ugly.[125]

Money

• Nineteenth-century political cartoonist Thomas Nast was fearless. He opposed William Magear Tweed — a corrupt New York politician known as "Boss" Tweed. The Tweed Ring of corrupt politicians got its money from kickbacks from contractors. For example, a contractor might be able to do a particular job for $30,000, but it would bid $100,000. Boss Tweed would make sure that particular contractor got the job, and in return the contractor would do the job for $30,000, keep $5,000 as profit for himself, and give Boss Tweed the remaining $65,000. Boss Tweed and his cronies kept themselves in office by giving recent immigrants citizenship, jobs, and other favors in return for their votes. (In 1868, Boss Tweed bought so many votes and had so many people vote multiple times for him that the number of votes cast was greater than the number of voters!) However, although the immigrants were illiterate, they could easily understand the critical cartoons that Mr. Nast drew about the corrupt Tweed Ring, and this worried Boss Tweed so much that he attempted to bribe Mr. Nast. A banker visited Mr. Nast one day and told him that a group of wealthy men who admired him wanted to give him $100,000 so he could go to Europe and study art instead of staying in New York and drawing political cartoons. Mr. Nast was suspicious, so he asked if the offer of money could be raised to $200,000. The banker replied that it could. Mr. Nast then asked if the offer could be raised to $500,000. The banker replied, "You can get five hundred thousand dollars in gold to drop this Ring business and get out of the country." Knowing that Boss Tweed was behind the offer to go to Europe and study art, Mr. Nast said, "Well, I don't think I'll do it. I made up my mind a long time ago to put some of those fellows behind bars, and I'm going to put them there." Mr. Nast did help bring down the Tweed Ring.[126]

• Carl Fabergé created many works of art for the Russian Imperial family, including his famous Easter eggs, but working for royalty did have its disadvantages. Alexandra, wife of Czar Nicholas, occasionally wanted Mr. Fabergé to create a piece of jewelry for her, so she would send a drawing to him along with a statement of how much she was willing to pay to have the artwork created. Unfortunately, she did not know much about goldsmithing, so Mr. Fabergé was often obliged to alter her drawing and her piece of jewelry. In addition, Mr. Fabergé sometimes took a loss in manufacturing one of her pieces of jewelry — no one would dare to suggest that the Czarina pay a higher price than the one she had suggested! Fortunately, Mr. Fabergé was able to make up the losses with the other work that he created for the Russian imperial family. (For example, Nicholas once gave Alexandra a diamond necklace that cost 166,500 rubles, and his parents once gave her a 267-pearl necklace that cost 171,600 rubles. Mr. Fabergé made both necklaces, and each necklace cost the equivalent of several hundred thousand dollars.)[127]

• While growing up, country comedian Archie Campbell liked to draw, and he quickly discovered that he enjoyed creating art a whole lot better than doing heavy farm work. As a youngster, he once worked an entire day pulling hay for 75 cents. The next day, he was so sore that he couldn't go to work and pull hay. That turned out to be a lucky break because a neighbor lady asked him to paint a picture on her wall. Archie painted the picture in three hours, and the neighbor lady was so pleased that she gave him $3 — a lot of money in those days. Archie raced home and told his mother that he had made in three hours as an artist what he would have made in four days as a hay puller. He also said that he was going to make his living as an artist. Things didn't quite work out that way, as Archie first became a country musician and then made it big as a country comedian, but he kept on painting — mostly as a hobby but occasionally as a source of income.[128]

• One would expect that the owner of an art gallery would be very aware of how much money a customer has available to spend on art, but it doesn't always work out that way. Before World War II, Lucy Carrington Wertheim ran an art gallery that concentrated on the work of then-modern artists. One day, a well-dressed woman expressed interest in a work of art by L.D. Rust — a drawing of a horse, which she wanted for her little son's room. Ms. Wertheim named the price, but the well-dressed woman returned the drawing to the portfolio. Because Ms. Wertheim thought that the price had been too high for the woman, she reduced it, and the well-dressed woman bought the drawing. Ms. Wertheim then discovered that the well-dressed woman was Barbara Hutton, Countess Reventlow, who at the time was the richest woman in the world.[129]

• Edna Hibel showed much talent early in her career, and of course people wanted to buy her paintings early in her career, causing a kind of crisis because she did not want to sell them. However, she talked to her art teacher, Professor Karl Zerbe, who gave her good advice. He told her that if she thought she could paint a better painting, then she ought to sell a painting she had already created, but if she thought she could not create a better painting, then she ought to hold on to the painting she thought was best. Of course, Ms. Hibel always thought she could create a better painting, so she began to sell her paintings. She says, "I hope I can always do better! Letting go of what I consider my best work is much easier when I remember Karl Zerbe's remarks."[130]

• When Andy Warhol was a successful commercial artist, but wanted to become a successful fine artist, he asked Muriel Latow, a friend and interior decorator, for her advice. However, her advice was not free. She asked for $50, and Mr. Warhol wrote her a check for $50. She then asked what he loved most in the world. The answer came back: "Money." Therefore, Ms. Latow advised him to paint money, and she also advised him to paint something that no one ever noticed because they were so familiar with it — "Something like a can of Campbell's soup." Mr. Warhol took her advice, and he remains famous as a pioneer of Pop Art.[131]

• To become an artist requires a great amount of effort over a great period of time. While on the witness stand during an action he had instituted against the critic John Ruskin, James McNeill Whistler was asked how long it had taken him to produce a certain painting. When the lawyer for the defense heard that Mr. Whistler had produced the painting in two days, he asked him, "The labor of two days, then, is that for which you ask two hundred guineas?" Mr. Whistler replied, "No, I ask it for the knowledge of a lifetime."[132]

• As a young man, African-American artist Henry Ossawa Tanner taught at Clark University in Atlanta, Georgia. Bishop and Mrs. Joseph Crane Hartzell took an interest in Mr. Tanner and his works of art and held an exhibition of his paintings. Unfortunately, the people who attended the exhibition purchased none of the paintings. Therefore, the Hartzells bought every painting. This raised enough money for Mr. Tanner to go to Paris, France, and study painting at the Academie Julien.[133]

• African-American artist Romare Bearden received money for attending his first year of college by working at a speakeasy during Prohibition. His job was collecting money from the waiters whose job was selling liquor. When the speakeasy was held up, the robber didn't get much money because most of the money was in Mr. Bearden's pants pockets. His boss was so happy that he gave Mr. Bearden a bonus — enough money to pay for his first year of college.[134]

• When Japanese painter and printmaker Katsushika Hokusai went bankrupt, he worried about getting art supplies. Sometimes he walked 15 miles after dark to Edo, where he would buy his art supplies while trying to stay hidden from anyone to whom he owed money. Nevertheless, he was unimpressed by anyone who had lots of money. Sometimes, he would keep a wealthy art collector waiting while he picked fleas off his clothing.[135]

• The young Pablo Picasso was in a junk shop one day when he came across a painting by Henri Rousseau and bought it. The junk dealer didn't think much of the painting and thought Picasso was buying it only to paint over the canvas, and so Picasso was able to buy the painting for approximately a dollar. The painting, *Portrait of a Woman*, is on display at the Musée Picasso in Paris — it is worth mega-bucks.[136]

• Sir David Wilkie sold his painting *Chelsea Pensioners Reading the Gazette of the Battle of Waterloo* for 1,000 guineas to the Duke of Wellington, who began to count out the banknotes. Sir David suggested that it might be easier to write out a draft on a banker, but the Duke of Wellington replied, "I don't want my bankers to know that I have been such a d*mned fool as to give 1,000 guineas for a painting."[137]

• In 1962, Andy Warhol exhibited his paintings of Campbell's soup cans at the Ferus Gallery in Los Angeles, California, charging $100 for each painting. An owner of a different, nearby art gallery saw the exhibit, was amused, and purchased several cans of Campbell's soup that he sold at his own gallery. The price of three cans was sixty cents, and a sign at the gallery advertised, "Buy them cheaper here."[138]

• James McNeill Whistler gave his paintings names such as *Arrangement in Black and White.* The secretary of his London club, wishing for Mr. Whistler to pay his long overdue membership fees, sent him this letter: "Dear Mr. Whistler: It is not a 'Nocturne in Purple' or a 'Symphony in Blue and Grey' we are after, but an 'Arrangement in Gold and Silver.'" Mr. Whistler paid the money he owed.[139]

• Mary Cassatt sometimes bullied her rich friends into buying art. One day, as she and multimillionaire James Stillman were looking at a painting by Diego Velasquez in René Gimpel's art gallery, she told him, "Buy it. It's shameful to be rich like you. Such a purchase will redeem you." He bought the painting.[140]

• As a movie producer, Louis B. Mayer was always interested in the bottom line. Once, Gottfried Reinhardt wanted to make a movie that Mr. Mayer felt had no commercial potential, so Mr. Mayer said to Mr. Reinhardt, "You want to be an artist, but you want other people to starve for your art."[141]

• Pablo Picasso often painted over the white walls of the apartments where he lived, turning them into works of art. Early in Picasso's career, an angry landlord forced him to pay to have a wall painted again. Years later, Picasso said, "What a fool. He could have sold the wall for a fortune."[142]

• Wilson Mizner once owned a store that sold reproductions of masterpiece paintings. After being offered $50 for a reproduction of Leonardo Da Vinci's *Last Supper*, he replied, "No, sir. It's worth ten dollars a plate, and I'm charging a hundred for the whole thing."[143]

• Before World War II, Lord Sandwich visited an art gallery owned by Lucy Carrington Wertheim. He liked what he saw very much, but he remarked that although he would like to buy some pictures from her, "Alas! I'll have to wait until I've paid my income tax."[144]

Mothers

• Cathy Guisewite, creator of the comic strip *Cathy*, became a successful cartoonist partly because of her mother. Ms. Guisewite used to send cartoons to her mother, who was so impressed that she researched a list of syndicates for her daughter to contact. Ms. Guisewite was afraid that her mother would contact the syndicates if she did not, so on 12 April 1976, she mailed a letter and some cartoons to Universal Press Syndicate. The executives there looked over her cartoons, discussed them, and 90 minutes after opening her package decided to syndicate her cartoon. Later, Ms. Guisewite joked that she had been "forced by Mother to send humiliating drawings of my miserable love life to Universal Press Syndicate."[145]

• When world-famous window dresser Simon Doonan was four years old, he threw his mother's bras out the window. When she asked him why he had done that, he replied, "Because they flutter." (Young Simon was effeminate and gay and interested in fabulous fashion. At the circus, he saw some ladies wearing fabulous and glittery costumes with plumes and asked his mother, "Why can't you dress like that?")[146]

Museums

• In the first half of the 1800s, George Catlin sought to paint Native Americans and Native American culture before their way of life was lost. Later, he sought to sell his Indian Gallery collection of paintings and artifacts of Native American life to the United States government but failed. However, much of his collection ended up in the Smithsonian anyway, donated to it by the heirs of Joseph Harrison, who purchased the Indian Gallery after it was sold to pay Mr. Catlin's debts. Ironically, it is a good thing that the U.S. government did not buy the Indian Gallery when it was offered for sale earlier. If the Indian Gallery had been put in the Smithsonian before 1865, it would have been burned up in a great fire that destroyed the Smithsonian building that year. By the way, although this next anecdote is not funny, it illustrates how much Mr. Catlin valued art. One day, after he had wounded a bull bison, he began to make sketches of it. After the wounded bull, near death, fell down, he threw his hat at it and harassed it until it got up again. He felt that such harassment of a dying animal was justified in order to make authentic sketches of the bison. Also by the way, in the old days, Western cowboys did not particularly care for people who didn't dress like them. A young man newly arrived from Boston once entered a saloon in a Western town while wearing a suit and patent leather shoes. A few minutes later, he emerged with a dazed look, wearing an undershirt and one sock. The cowboys inside had resented his clothing, ordered him to buy a round of drinks, and when he said that all he had was 25 cents, had stripped him and pawned his clothes to pay for the drinks.[147]

• For many years, Carl Fabergé created an Easter egg for the Czar of Russia to give to his wife. Each Easter egg, when opened, contained a surprise, such as a model of the Czar's private train or a model of the Czar's yacht or a model of the coach in which the Czarina had ridden to a coronation. The surprise was a surprise to everyone, even to the Czar, who had commissioned the work of art. Once the Czar asked Mr. Fabergé what surprise he was planning, and Mr. Fabergé would tell him only, "Your Imperial majesty will be satisfied." He was. (By the way, a woman once asked Mr. Fabergé this silly question: "What shape will your eggs have this year?" He joked, "Madam, this year they will be square!") Today, any museum with a Fabergé Easter egg is a proud museum.[148]

• Many horticulturalists work at the National Gallery of Art in Washington, D.C. They care for the plants used in the exhibits, and they sometimes notice things in paintings that other people don't notice. For example, Rembrandt Peale's portrait of Rubens Peale, his teenage brother, includes a geranium. Museum horticulturalists look at the painting and wish that Rubens Peale would water the geranium.[149]

Chapter 4: From Music to Prejudice

Music

• Throughout his life, jazz musician Louis Armstrong made collages about events that were important to him. Many of his collages concerned events from his personal life, but other collages were about events that made history. For example, one collage was created from newspaper clippings telling how Jackie Robinson broke the color barrier in modern major-league professional baseball. A study of the collages, many of which are on display at Queens College in New York City, shows that Mr. Armstrong followed closely the advances African Americans were making in civil rights.[150]

• Music has no fans like punk fans. Richard Hell designed a T-shirt with a bull's-eye target and the words "Please kill me" on it. Richard Lloyd, lead guitarist of the punk group Television, once wore the T-shirt. Some wild-eyed punk fans saw the T-shirt and told him, "If that's what you want, we'll be happy to oblige because we're such big fans!" Immediately, Mr. Lloyd thought, "I am NOT wearing this shirt again."[151]

Names

• Dahlia Messick wanted to be a cartoonist, but she noticed that when she took her artwork around to the studios that the male decision-makers would only briefly look at her artwork but would ask her out to lunch. Therefore, she adopted the gender-neutral name *Dale* Messick and started mailing her artwork to studios. Eventually, she created the very successful comic strip *Brenda Starr, Reporter*.[152]

• In 1969, Charlie Brown and Snoopy became the mascots of the Apollo 10 Lunar exploration crew. The lunar module received the nickname "Snoopy," and the command module received the nickname "Charlie Brown." When the lunar module and the command module had redocked, the astronauts reported to Mission Control, "Snoopy and Charlie Brown are hugging each other."[153]

• Magazines aren't always totally honest about who writes for them. For example, early in its history, *Ms.* magazine published a comic strip titled *Mary Selfworth*. Supposedly, the comic strip was written and drawn by Vincenza Colletta; however, the real writer and drawer was a Marvel cartoonist named Vincent Colletta.[154]

• Neysa McMein was a painter whose career went nowhere when she painted under her real name, Marjorie Moran McMein. After she changed her name to the one suggested by a numerologist, she became successful.[155]

Opinions

• Many Impressionist artists painted landscapes outdoors, but Edgar Degas preferred to paint indoor scenes of entertainers such as ballet dancers or singers. A landscape artist once asked him whether such subjects were suitable for art, and Mr. Degas replied, "For you, natural life is necessary; for me, artificial life." (Actually, Mr. Degas disliked painters who worked outdoors. He once said, "If I were in the government, I would have a brigade of policemen assigned to keeping an eye on people who paint landscapes outdoors. Oh, I wouldn't want anyone killed. I'd be satisfied with just a few buckshot to begin with.")[156]

• Cathy Guisewite, the creator of the comic strip *Cathy*, keeps an 8-Ball — one of those contraptions that answers questions with "Yes," "No," "Maybe," and so on — in her office. She says that although it doesn't make decisions for her, "It's good to get a second opinion."[157]

Painting

• Mexican artist Diego Rivera well remembered the first time he saw a painting by Paul Cézanne. While in Paris, Mr. Rivera passed a gallery that had a painting by Mr. Cézanne displayed in a window. Mr. Rivera looked at the painting for one hour and then for another hour. The owner of the gallery saw Mr. Rivera looking at the painting, so he put a different painting by Mr. Cézanne on display in the window. Mr. Rivera looked at that painting for hours, so the art gallery owner placed a third painting by Mr. Cézanne on display. Mr. Rivera was still looking at the painting when closing time for the gallery came, so the owner then placed several paintings by Mr. Cézanne in the window and went home. Mr. Rivera stayed yet longer to look at the paintings, getting soaked in a rainstorm. When he went home, he was feverish, and visions of paintings by Mr. Cézanne kept running through his head. Some of the paintings were real; some were imaginary.[158]

• When she was a child, ballerina Tanaquil Le Clercq used to look at the painting *Sacred and Profane Love* and wonder which figure represented Sacred Love: the fully clothed figure, or the nude figure? She was told that the nude figure symbolized virtue. Therefore, she was looking forward to dancing the role of Sacred Love in Sir Frederick Ashton's ballet *Illuminations* — to be relatively unclothed is a blessing to a dancer, as too much costuming interferes with the ability to dance. Unfortunately, Sacred Love wore a lot of costuming in the ballet, whereas Profane Love wore much less costuming. In fact, the ballerina dancing the role of Profane Love wore one ballet slipper instead of two. However, this turned out not to be a blessing, as the ballerina frequently forgot which foot was shod and in going up on pointe with the unshod foot, she bruised all five toenails, resulting in some unballerina-like cursing in the wings.[159]

• When trains were new inventions, Impressionist Claude Monet created paintings of them. He became friends with a stationmaster who helped him paint the trains. For example, the stationmaster would reschedule trains to enable Mr. Monet to finish a painting. In addition, the stationmaster would have the train engineers release clouds of white smoke so that Mr. Monet could paint them.[160]

• Movie director Peter Bogdanovich's father was an artist who would not sign a painting until after it was sold. He once went to the home of a person who had bought a painting and brought a palette so that he could sign it. Half an hour later, the art collector looked in the room where the painting was and discovered the artist busily repainting the work of art.[161]

• Clementine Hunter was a self-taught African-American folk artist who painted after all her other work was done. Often, she painted at night while her husband, Emmanuel, tried to sleep. One night, he told her, "Woman, if you don't stop painting and get some sleep, you'll sure go crazy." She replied, "No, if I don't get this painting out of my head, I'll sure go crazy."[162]

• The most famous painting in the world is perhaps Leonardo da Vinci's *Mona Lisa*. After he died, it became the possession of King Francis I of France. French royalty owned the painting for centuries, although they didn't always choose to hang it in a place that art lovers would consider appropriate. For a while, the *Mona Lisa* was displayed in the royal bathroom![163]

• When Paul Cézanne was 13 years old, he rescued a skinny, near-sighted kid named Émile Zola from bullies. To show his gratitude, the future novelist gave the future painter a basket filled with apples. As an adult, Mr. Cézanne frequently painted apples and once declared, "I wish to conquer Paris with an apple."[164]

• Impressionist painter Edgar Degas regarded gold frames as garish and in bad taste. At a dinner party, he discovered one of his paintings in a gold frame. He waited until he was alone, and then he took his painting out of the frame, rolled up the canvas, put it under his arm, and left the party, carrying away the painting.[165]

• Some great art is painted on ordinary surfaces. In his 1889 work titled *Self-Portrait with Halo*, Paul Gauguin depicted himself as the Fallen Angel. The work was created at Marie Henry's inn in Le Pouldu. Mr. Gauguin painted it in the dining room directly on wooden cupboard doors.[166]

• In the first half of the 17th century, Artemisia Gentileschi of Italy was a painter who knew her own worth. Once she sent a painting to a patron, along with this note: "This will show your Lordship what a woman can do."[167]

People with Handicaps

• While fighting in World War I as a member of the African-American Hell Fighters of the 369th Regiment, painter Horace Pippin was wounded by a German sniper as he dove into a shell hole. A French soldier came by, looked in the hole, and then was shot by the sniper and fell dead on top of Mr. Pippin, who had lost so much blood that he was unable to move the French soldier off of himself. Eventually, Mr. Pippin was rescued, and a steel plate was put in his right shoulder. Of course, his right arm was weak and stiff after the injury, and it looked as if he would never create art again. However, at home one day he noticed a poker resting in the fire that kept his house warm. The tip of the poker was white-hot, and Mr. Pippin discovered that he could hold the cool end of the poker with his right arm, rest the poker on his knee, and create a burnt drawing by using his left arm to hold a wooden plank up to the white-hot poker. He managed to create several burnt-wood panels that way, including his first: *Losing the Way*.[168]

• In 1897, José Clemente Orozco was a 14-year-old boy (some sources say he was 21) living in Mexico City, Mexico. Like other boys his age, he was curious about fireworks and gunpowder, and when he was alone one day, he experimented. Suddenly, the gunpowder exploded, blowing three fingers off his left hand and also badly injuring his right hand. Young Clemente ended up having his left hand amputated, and he nearly lost his right hand as well. In addition, his sight and hearing were damaged. For the rest of his life, he was forced to wear thick glasses, and he never regained hearing in his left ear. Nevertheless, he became one of Mexico's foremost painters, gaining special renown for his murals. In 1947, he won Mexico's National Prize in the Arts and Sciences, and when he died in 1949, he was given the honor of burial in the *Rotunda de los Hombres Illustres* (Rotunda of the Illustrious Men).[169]

• Al Capp, creator of the comic strip *Li'l Abner*, had a wooden leg, which occasionally created embarrassing situations for him. One morning, at the Savoy Hotel in London, he lay in bed as a waiter took his breakfast order. Because Mr. Capp was well covered with bedding, the waiter could not tell that he had only one leg, but the waiter did notice the foot of Mr. Capp's wooden leg, clothed in a shoe and a stocking, sticking out from under the bed. In fact, the waiter stared at it. Becoming aware that Mr. Capp was watching him stare at the leg, the waiter recovered his composure, finished taking Mr. Capp's order, and then said, "Very good, sir. And what will the other gentleman have?"[170]

• Henri de Toulouse-Lautrec, the little person who became a great Impressionist painter, once did a series of lithographs featuring singer Yvette Guilbert, who was not beautiful. As Ms. Guilbert looked over the lithographs, she noticed that Mr. Toulouse-Lautrec had made some things grotesque, and so she said to him, "Really, you have a genius for depicting deformity!" He replied, "But of course."[171]

Photography

• As a wildlife photographer, M. Timothy O'Keefe had to be a patient man, as it took days or weeks to photograph the scenes he wanted. He also had to be quick, as taking the actual photograph took a fraction of a second. To focus his camera ahead of time, he used to tape his driver license to something in the scene he would photograph, such as a tree limb, focus on the license, and then remove it. In 1979, he wanted to photograph an owl with a freshly caught mouse, so he picked a tree branch where an owl might enjoy a meal, focused his camera, and then waited in a blind. One night, he heard a squeak of a mouse and then the owl settling on the branch. He tripped the shutter, four strobe lights illuminated the branch, and he had the photograph he wanted. Well, almost. Yes, he had photographed the owl and the mouse, but he had also photographed his driver license, which he had forgotten to remove from the tree limb.[172]

• For several months, Albert E. Kahn photographed Soviet ballerina Galina Ulanova, but he is aware that his photographs record only a small part of her career — a career that has not been much recorded in photographs. He asked a Soviet photographer why more photographs were not taken of her, and the Soviet replied, "You know how it is when you are very close to something beautiful, so close that you can reach out and touch it with your hand? You sometimes tend to take that beauty for granted, as if it will always be there."[173]

• *MAD* occasionally uses photographs in its satires. Originally, the photographers — creators for *MAD* — used professional models, but the models were unable to pose satirically. This led the *MAD* creators to grimace and make funny faces to illustrate what they wanted the models to do. Eventually, someone figured out that they could get better photographs and save money by using *MAD* people, including *MAD* publisher William M. Gaines, in the photographs instead of professional models.[174]

• At the 1998 American Choreography Awards show, Rose Eichenbaum went up to choreographer Daniel Ezralow and told him, "I am a talented photographer and would very much like to photograph you. Do you think that would be possible?" He told her, "I'm sure you are, and I'll be happy to work with you." He also gave her his private telephone number. The photo shoot went well, and they became friends. He later told her that he had to take her seriously because of how bold she had been.[175]

• Christina Lessa is a renowned photographer of gymnasts. As such, she must be very persuasive and very creative. For example, her 1997 book, *Gymnastics Balancing Acts*, includes photographs of a barefoot Shannon Miller standing on top of a horse during a cold winter day, Dominique Dawes balancing near the edge of the top of a Times Square skyscraper, and Trent Dimas jumping near a steep incline by the Statue of Liberty.[176]

• Ron Protas is renowned for his photographs of famous dancers and choreographers, including a silhouette photograph of Martha Graham in her old age sitting on a stool. He was always unfailingly polite. Whenever he was asked to leave a performance because he was taking photographs, he would chuckle and then leave by a door — and re-enter by another door so he could take more photographs.[177]

• In the days before Photoshop, portrait painting had at least one advantage over portrait photography. Queen Victoria once asked court painter Alfred Chalfont, whether photography would replace painting. The Frenchman replied, *"Ah, non, Madame! Photographie* can't *flattère."*[178]

• Berenice Abbott wanted to go to the Bowery to take a few photographs, but a supervisor tried to stop her from going by telling her that nice girls did not go to the Bowery. She replied that she was a photographer — not a nice girl.[179]

Portraits

• Wandering artists in the American frontier days used to make money by painting portraits with no faces. The portraits might be of one person, a married couple, or even an entire family, and the people in the portraits wore fancy, expensive clothing. The artist then traveled around, showing settlers the portraits. If a settler liked one, the artist would then paint in the face of the settler, or of the settler and his wife, or even the settler's entire family, depending on which portrait the settler bought. Thus, many settlers owned portraits showing them wearing clothing they had never worn.[180]

• Paul Cézanne was an Impressionist perfectionist. He made Ambroise Vollard sit 115 times while creating his portrait. When the portrait was finished, Mr. Cézanne declared that its only satisfactory part was the front of Mr. Vollard's shirt.[181]

• Romaine Brooks painted many celebrities. She found it difficult to get Jean Couteau to sit so she could paint him until she discovered his weakness — she bribed him with pieces of chocolate cake.[182]

• Actress Sarah Siddons' nose was somewhat longer than usual. When Thomas Gainsborough painted her portrait, he exclaimed, "D*mn it, madam, there is no end to your nose!"[183]

Practical Jokes

• Mike Balukas was an artist at the Walt Disney studios in the early days. He was deaf, so he was unable to hear people shouting "Earthquake!" in times when people had an urgent need to shout "Earthquake!" in order to get other people out of buildings that might quickly collapse. Therefore, Mr. Balukas used to place a number of short pencil stubs on top of his desk. When an earthquake occurred, the pencil stubs fell onto his drawing board, and he knew to get out of the building — quickly. Recognizing an opportunity when they saw it, other Disney employees would sometimes sneak into a room that shared a wall with Mr. Balukas' room, and they would bang on the wall until the pencil stubs fell onto Mr. Balukas' drawing board, sending him running for safety.[184]

• Old money doesn't like new money. That is what Alva Smith discovered when she married William K. Vanderbilt in the 1870s. Although Mr. Vanderbilt had approximately $100 million, they were 100 million *new* dollars, and so old money did not especially care for the Vanderbilts. However, Mrs. Vanderbilt wanted to climb the social strata, and so she hired an architect to design a $3 million mansion for her and her husband. Unfortunately, the architect she hired was Richard M. Hunt, whose idea of a private joke was to build her a replica of the mansion of Jacques Coeur, a famous 15th-century social climber.[185]

• Children's book illustrator Victoria Chess owned two cats, Zazou and Pearl, which liked to play practical jokes on her pet dog. Working together, Zazou and Pearl would capture a chipmunk and carry it into the house, where they would release it near the dog. They then would sit back and watch the dog explode into a furniture-upheaving frenzy.[186]

• Practical joker Hugh Troy once painted a mural for the Bowery Savings Bank in New York City. The mural depicted the New York port in the heyday of the clipper ships. In the foreground was a clipper ship with its mast filled with signal flags. Deciphered, the signal flags read, "Keep your money in your mattress."[187]

Prejudice

• American artist Romare Bearden was light-skinned and could have passed for white if he had wished. In fact, when he was a young man, he was a good baseball player and could have passed for white in the white-only major leagues if he had wished; however, he had absolutely no wish to pass for white. One day, when he was three years old, his parents took him shopping in the white section of Charlotte, North Carolina. His mother went into a store, and his father left young Romare in their horse-drawn carriage for a moment to look in a store window. When his father came back to fair-skinned Romare in the carriage, white people were shocked and thought that he was a kidnapper. Soon afterward, his family moved to New York City, where they hoped to find a less racist area of America.[188]

• In the 1920s, Oliver W. Harrington and one other boy were the only black students in a South Bronx 6th-grade class. One day, their teacher, Miss McCoy, called them to the front of the classroom, pointed her finger at them, and told the white students, "Never, never forget that these two belong in that there trash basket." Mr. Harrington says that the white students laughed in what "must have been their first trip on the racist drug." After that experience, Mr. Harrington began to draw caricatures of Miss McCoy (showing such things as a train running over her), and he became a famous black cartoonist who published several collections of his work.[189]

• In 1951, Marty Links, cartoonist of *Teena*, was nominated to become the first woman member of the National Cartoonist Society. She was blackballed. Why? The reason given was that the men wanted to "talk dirty" and they couldn't do that in the presence of a woman.

Protests followed. Al Capp, cartoonist of *Li'l Abner*, walked out — six years later, following changes for the better in the NCS, he returned. Milton Caniff, cartoonist of *Terry and the Pirates*, made a speech supporting Ms. Links, and definitely not supporting the people who had blackballed her. Eventually, Ms. Links became a member in good standing, and she promptly nominated two other women cartoonists for membership in the NCS.[190]

• Edward Mitchell Bannister was an important early African-American artist, and he faced prejudice. When he heard that his painting titled *Under the Oaks* had won a prize at the Centennial Exposition of 1876 in Philadelphia, Pennsylvania, he wanted to confirm this information, so he made his way through a crowd of people at the exhibition. While doing so, he heard someone say, "Why is this colored person here?" When he reached the inquiry desk, he was ignored, and when he finally was able to ask if *Under the Oaks* had won a prize, the man at the inquiry desk asked, "What's that to you?" Mr. Bannister replied, "I painted that picture." (His painting won the bronze medal.)[191]

• When she was a college student, Maya Lin, whose ancestry is Chinese, traveled to Denmark. When she sat down on a bus, the people sitting near her got up, moved away from her, and sat down again. Later, Ms. Lin designed the Vietnam Veterans Memorial on the Mall in Washington, D.C.[192]

Chapter 5: From Problem-Solving to Work

Problem-Solving

• American artist Romare Bearden once ran into a creative block and was unable to paint. One day, his housekeeper asked if the unpainted piece of brown paper that was lying on his easel was the same unpainted piece of brown paper that she had seen there the previous week. It was, and Mr. Bearden confessed that he was suffering from a creative block. Fortunately, the housekeeper, a plain woman whom one of Mr. Bearden's friends had called so ugly that "she looked like a locomotive coming around a corner," had the solution: "Why don't you paint me? I know what I look like, but when you look and find what's beautiful in me, then you're going to be able to do something on that paper of yours." The suggestion worked. Mr. Bearden painted her, and then he continued to create many great works of art.[193]

• Clementine Hunter was a self-taught African-American folk artist who sold her paintings to buy some of the necessities (and some of the luxuries) of life such as a stove, refrigerator, freezer, mobile home, secondhand car, radio, and television. Because of a lack of money, she sometimes thinned her paint with turpentine, and she often painted on pieces of board and on plastic milk jugs. Eventually, she became well known as an artist, and celebrity seekers started trying to visit her. She didn't especially enjoy meeting strangers, and when a car of celebrity seekers came by, she would tell them, "Clementine Hunter? She lives just on down the road a piece." After her death, one of her works of art — a window shade she had painted — sold for $60,000.[194]

• Because Winslow Homer was a famous artist, lots of people wished to visit him in his studio. However, because Mr. Homer was a hard-working artist, he wished to be alone in his studio so he could paint. Therefore, to ward off unwelcome visitors, on the door of his studio he painted these words: "Coal Bin." Of course, his friends were welcome to visit him. These friends used a code knock to gain entrance to his studio. When they knocked three times, Mr. Homer opened the door. A different number of knocks, and Mr. Homer kept the door closed. Of course, Mr. Homer couldn't avoid all unwelcome visitors. When he could, he ran away and hid; when he couldn't run and hide, he pretended to be not himself, but his servant.[195]

• The very wealthy merchant Su once brought a large and valuable pearl to a skilled jeweler named Czu and asked him to drill a hole in it so that it could be made part of a necklace. However, Czu examined the pearl and said, "This pearl is much too valuable for me to risk ruining it." Therefore, Su took the pearl to another skilled jeweler, Li-jo, and asked him to drill a hole in it. Li-jo examined the pearl, realized its great value, and called an apprentice over and told him to drill a hole in the pearl. The apprentice did so quickly and perfectly. Su asked Li-jo why he had entrusted such a valuable pearl to a mere apprentice. Li-jo replied, "He does not know how valuable the pearl is, and so his hands didn't shake when he drilled a hole in it."[196]

• Sculptor Louise Nevelson once created a retrospective exhibition at New York City's Whitney Museum of American Art. Because it was a retrospective exhibition, it included some of her early work — including work she was no longer proud of. One piece that she especially disliked was a sculpture titled *Earth Figure*. A friend of hers was helping to move the works of art around the gallery, and as he was moving *Earth Figure*, she suddenly yelled, "Drop it!" Startled, he did drop it, and the sculpture shattered on the floor. Later, the friend — her biographer Arnold Glimcher — wrote, "She was now satisfied with the exhibition; she had edited out the weakest piece."[197]

• Late in life, after Leonardo da Vinci had become very famous and was working at the Vatican, uninvited visitors often interrupted his work. To get rid of unwanted visitors, he turned his pet lizard into a monster by gluing a horn to its head and bat-like wings to its back. He also created glittering spots on its back, perhaps by using fish scales. Leonardo asked unwanted visitors if they would like to see a curiosity, and when they replied yes, Leonardo let the lizard out of a box. The lizard scurried to the visitors, and the visitors scurried to the nearest exit.[198]

• Ham Fisher created the comic strip *Joe Palooka* and took some sample panels to McNaught Newspaper Syndicate, which was not interested in the strip but offered him a job selling comic strips to newspapers. Mr. Fisher accepted the job, and he traveled from newspaper to newspaper selling various comic strips to them, including *Joe Palooka*, which he pretended the syndicate was offering. When he returned to the home office, he had 20 newspapers signed up to carry *Joe Palooka* and the syndicate decided to carry it.[199]

• When Arthur Yorinks and Richard Egielski decided to collaborate on a children's picture-book titled *Louis the Fish*, author Yorinks wrote that Louis was a salmon. However, illustrator Egielski didn't know how to draw a salmon, so he went to a grocery store, where he found a picture of one on the label of a can of salmon. Since he watched his money carefully in those days, he didn't buy the can, but instead tore off the label and smuggled it out of the store. Mr. Egielski says, "The salmon on that can is what I used to draw Louis."[200]

• When Robert McCloskey was creating his picture-book *Make Way for Ducklings*, he bought and kept six ducklings in his bathtub so he could sketch them. One problem he ran into was that the ducklings were so active that he found it difficult to sketch them, so he needed to find a way to slow them down. Eventually, he discovered the solution to his problem — red wine. The ducklings loved the wine, and it made them so mellow that they moved in slow motion.[201]

• A nobleman once commissioned William Hogarth to paint his portrait, which Mr. Hogarth did, but then the nobleman refused to accept and pay for the painting. Mr. Hogarth wrote the nobleman, saying that unless the portrait was paid for, he would add a tail and other such embellishments to the portrait and then sell it to an exhibitor of wild beasts. The threat worked — Mr. Hogarth received the money the nobleman owed him.[202]

• Comedian Anita Wise was in a store, looking at miniature paintings on very small boxes. She wasn't interested in buying anything, just looking, but a salesman began talking to her about the miniature paintings, pointing out that the artists had created them by using a single camel hair as a brush. Ms. Wise asked, "Why don't they just get bigger boxes?"[203]

• One winter, Impressionist painter Claude Monet started painting a tree without leaves. Unfortunately, he had not finished painting the tree when spring arrived and leaves appeared on the tree. In order to finish his painting, he paid the owner of the tree 50 francs to remove all of its leaves. In May, Mr. Monet finished his painting.[204]

• Spanish painter Francisco Goya usually painted in the bright light of the morning, but he sometimes did a few finishing touches at night. Electric lights had not yet been invented, so he painted by candlelight. In fact, while painting at night he often wore a hat that had a rim set with metal brackets to hold candles.[205]

• The show must go on. Painter Georges Rouault was behind schedule in creating the costumes and sets for the premiere of George Balanchine's *Prodigal Son* by the Ballets Russes. Members of Ballets Russes locked Mr. Rouault in a room until he had finished the costumes and sets.[206]

• Renaissance painters and sculptors often showed draped clothing in their art. So that a model would not have to pose for hours while the artists worked on the draped clothing, the artists would take cloth, soak it in plaster, pose it and let it harden to serve as their model.[207]

• Watanabe Kazan, a samurai and a painter, was once placed under house arrest and ordered not to paint. Because he needed the income that he derived from painting, he continued to paint, but added earlier dates to his paintings to fool the authorities.[208]

Revenge

• Al Capp, creator of *Li'l Abner*, once hosted a party for a group of South American cartoonists. Unfortunately, he discovered that none of them could speak English. This meant that the only English-speaking people were himself, his brother, a few members of the State Department who wanted to foster greater understanding between North and South Americans, and fellow cartoonist Walt Kelly, creator of *Pogo*. Mr. Capp got tired of his party, so he and his brother ducked out, leaving Mr. Kelly to host the non-English-speaking South American cartoonists. Mr. Kelly responded with a creative act of revenge. He found an interpreter, and he told one of the South American cartoonists that Mr. Capp had told him that it was his dearest wish that the cartoonist be given his baby grand piano. When Mr. Capp arrived back home, he discovered his baby grand being lowered from his living-room window to the street below so it could be moved to a ship and taken to South America.[209]

• Hugh Troy was once summoned along with some other artists to the estate of a wealthy society lady who was holding an auction — attendance by invitation only (in other words, only rich people are welcome) — to raise money for a charity to benefit something or other. When the artists arrived, she told them, "I am giving you just two minutes of my time. You are each to paint a picture for the auction." When Mr. Troy asked if the artists were allowed to attend the party after their work was done, the society lady said, "No." Then the society lady ordered a servant to take the artists to a place with art materials they could use to paint pictures for the charity auction. However, Mr. Troy was annoyed at the woman, so instead of painting a picture he painted these signs: "Picnic Parties Welcome," "Welcome to the Carnival!" and "Free Rides! Bring the Kiddies!" Then he displayed the signs all around the entrance to the woman's estate, and left.[210]

• In Cedar Rapids, Iowa, Grant Wood received a commission from the American Legion to create a stained-glass window. Unfortunately, the Daughters of the American Revolution made a big stink when they discovered that the glass had been made in Germany, the United States' enemy in the then-recent World War I. (By the way, Mr. Wood had served in the U.S. Army.) The DAR wrote indignant letters and made indignant speeches. Mr. Wood got revenge later when he painted a portrait of three sour-faced women — he titled it *Daughters of the American Revolution*.[211]

Sculpture

• Maya Lin designed the Vietnam Veterans Memorial on the Mall in Washington, D.C., as the result of an assignment by Professor Andrus Burr of Yale University. He gave everyone in his class the guidelines of the contest to design the Memorial — it had to include the names of all the Americans killed or missing in action during the Vietnam War, and it had to be in harmony with the landscape and monuments of the Mall. Of all the students in the class, Ms. Lin was the only one to submit her design to the Vietnam Veterans Memorial Fund. Her design consisted of two walls that sank into the ground and then rose again. The names of the Vietnam dead and MIAs were engraved on the two walls. In addition, the walls were made of highly polished black marble to give a reflection of the Mall and of the people looking at the walls. Although Ms. Lin's design was the unanimous winner of the contest, when she had submitted her design to Professor Burr, he felt that it was "too strong" and gave it a B. However, Professor Burr encouraged Ms. Lin to submit her design to the VVMF, and he made two important suggestions concerning her design, both of which she accepted. He suggested that the two walls come together and form an angle, and he suggested that the names on the wall be arranged by date of death rather than by alphabetical order — a stroke of genius that Ms. Lin says kept the wall from looking "like a telephone book engraved in granite."[212]

• The statue of Abraham Lincoln inside the Lincoln Memorial in Washington, D.C. depicts Lincoln sitting. That is the result of a conscious decision made by its sculptor, Daniel Chester French. The statue is inside a building created by architect Henry Bacon, and the building resembles the Parthenon, a Greek temple with huge vertical marble pillars. If the statue were to depict Lincoln standing up, the impact of his figure would be lost among all the other vertical lines. Of course, Mr. French made many other artistic decisions when creating his statue of Lincoln. For example, one foot is forward, while the other is close to the chair Lincoln is sitting on. One of Lincoln's hands is open, while the other is closed. In addition, one of Mr. Lincoln's hands has a tapping finger because Mr. French noticed that Mr. Lincoln was using a finger to tap while talking to his generals in a photograph taken by Matthew Brady.[213]

• Pablo Picasso was a genius when it came to art, and he could create works of art from things other people regarded as junk. In 1942, he took a discarded bicycle seat and pair of handlebars and created a sculpture he called *Bull's Head*, which he then cast in bronze. In 1943, Picasso described *Bull's Head* to photographer George Brassaï: "Guess how I made the bull's head? One day, in a pile of objects all jumbled up together, I found an old bicycle seat right next to a rusty set of handlebars. In a flash, they joined together in my head. The idea of the Bull's Head came to me before I had a chance to think. All I did was weld them together... [but] if you were only to see the bull's head and not the bicycle seat and handlebars that form it, the sculpture would lose some of its impact."[214]

Surrealism

• Surrealists André Breton and Jacques Vaché used to go to movie theaters, but they ignored whatever movie was showing. Instead, they brought wine and food and had a picnic while everyone else watched the movie. However, Mr. Vaché occasionally attended plays for real. If he liked a play that the audience hated, he would threaten to shoot the members of the audience. (Perhaps unsurprisingly, Mr. Vaché died of an opium overdose.)[215]

• In 1938, when surrealism was new and few people knew what it was, comedian Gracie Allen had an exhibition of her paintings at a prestigious New York gallery. According to George Burns, her husband, everyone knew Gracie was a surrealist painter because no one understood her paintings, many of which had titles such as "Man Beholds a Better Mouse Trap and Buys a Mohair Toupée." Later, the exhibition went on a U.S. tour.[216]

Telephones

• Theodore Geisel, aka Dr. Seuss, used to live in an apartment near a fish store. His telephone number was one digit different from the telephone number of the fish store, and he used to occasionally get wrong numbers from people ordering fish. When that happened, he drew a picture of the order — say, two haddock — on a piece of cardboard from his laundry service and sent it to the fish store along with the rest of the order information.[217]

• Dick Sears worked at the Walt Disney studios in the early days as head of the Story department. He once saw an unusual name in the telephone and decided to make a call: "Hello, is this Gisella Werberserk Piffl? ... I'm an old friend of your brother's. We were classmates at Cornell. ... Oh, you've never had a brother who attended Cornell? I'm sorry — you must be some other Gisella Werberserk Piffl."[218]

Television

• On *The Dick Van Dyke Show*, the episode "October Eve" is about a painting that has Laura Petrie's head, but the nude body of another woman. (The character Laura Petrie was played by Mary Tyler Moore.) The episode was based on a real-life experience of writer Bill Persky, who had gone to an art gallery and seen a painting that closely resembled his wife. Jerry Paris, who played Jerry Helper on the series, had a similar experience. He and his wife had visited a prison, where a prisoner had sketched his wife's face. After they had left the prison, the prisoner used his imagination to create a nude drawing of Mrs. Paris and then sent it to their home as a present.[219]

• Being a commercial artist has its perks. Elmer Lehnhardt was hired to create the artwork used to decorate a children's lunchbox featuring scenes from the TV series *Land of the Giants*, starring a crew of American astronauts who land on a planet of giants. One side of the lunchbox showed the American space crew being menaced by a giant man — the face of the giant was a self-portrait by Mr. Lehnhardt.[220]

Theater

• Despite his profession, 19th-century cartoonist Bernhard Gillam took a serious view of life. Eugene Zimmerman, a friend and fellow cartoonist, once took him to see a comic play. While the other members of the audience laughed, Mr. Gillam scowled. After the play was over and they were leaving the theater, Mr. Gillam turned to Mr. Zimmerman and said, "If you ever dare to take me to see such rot again, I'll kill you."[221]

• For a Sunday newspaper, Sam Norkin once created a caricature for the opening of a play titled *All You Need is One Good Break*. Unfortunately, the critics hated the play, and it closed Saturday night. Sy Peck, editor of the New York *Compass*, decided to run the caricature anyway, with the heading "*All You Need is One Good Break* got no break from the critics."[222]

• When children's book illustrator Denise Fleming was a young girl, she and the neighborhood kids sometimes put on plays, charging other kids buttons for admission. Her young neighbor Charlie once tore all the buttons off his shirt so he could pay for himself and his friends to attend one of the plays.[223]

• Fire inspectors in the world of dance can terrify art lovers. For example, fire inspectors test scenery for fireproofing by attempting to set it on fire. Ballet dancer Frank Moncion moaned when he saw the fire inspectors test the setting for the ballet *Firebird* — it had been designed by Marc Chagall.[224]

Travel

• Joseph H. Meyers, at one time an English instructor at Purdue, was annoyed by bad guides when he toured Europe. He and his wife were able to get rid of the guides by being annoying. When a guide tried to tell the Meyers about Raphael's *Wedding of the Virgin*, Mrs. Meyers said, "Raphael was an American." The guide, of course, said, "No, no!" However, Mr. Meyers backed up his wife: "Raphael was born in Philadelphia." His wife then added, "We knew him personally." Eventually, the guide decided to leave them alone.[225]

• Late in life, Spanish painter Francisco Goya lived for a while in France. Of course, for long periods of time — including during much of Mr. Goya's lifetime — France and Spain have not been friendly, and the French police watched Mr. Goya for a time. Eventually, they decided that he was not a spy because he was so deaf and he was not able to cause trouble because his command of the French language was so poor.[226]

• Toller Cranston was both a Canadian figure skater and an artist. Once, he was performing in Wichita, Kansas, where he stayed in a hotel room with okra and mustard paintings on the wall. However, before he could sleep there, he demanded that the paintings be removed from his room. Why? He told the management, "I simply couldn't spend the weekend with them."[227]

• *MAD* publisher William M. Gaines used to take the *MAD* writers and artists on a trip every year or two. One year, he took everybody to Rome, and they visited the Sistine Chapel, where a tour guide informed them that Michelangelo had spent 15 years painting the ceiling. *MAD* writer Dick DeBartolo explained why: "Yeah, but it was *two* coats!"[228]

• During World War II, artist Marc Chagall left France to escape the Nazi invasion. He went to the United States, where unfortunately he refused to learn English. For a long time, Mr. Chagall refused to leave France for the United States, in part because of a lack of understanding about the country. In fact, he once asked, "Are there trees and cows in America, too?"[229]

War

• Mathew B. Brady is famous because of many Civil War photographs; however, from 1858, he began to suffer from poor eyesight and relied on other photographers to focus his camera, although he set up the shot. During the Civil War, he got permission from President Abraham Lincoln to photograph the war, and he trained many photographers to help him do that. After the Battle of Gettysburg, Mr. Brady and several photographers whom he had trained took photographs of the corpses on the battlefield. If it were needed to make a photograph more dramatic, they would change the position of a corpse. Did Mr. Brady take all the photographs that have been attributed to him? Probably not. He took credit for all the photographs that the men he had trained took — something that did not make him popular with these photographers.[230]

• Charles M. Schulz, creator of the comic strip *Peanuts*, was a soldier in World War II, but fortunately saw little action. He once saw a German soldier crossing the field, so he aimed his rifle at him and pulled the trigger. The rifle did not fire — Mr. Schulz had not loaded it due to forgetfulness. Fortunately, the German soldier surrendered. Mr. Schulz also once thought some German soldiers were in an artillery emplacement, so he got ready to throw a grenade into the emplacement. However, he saw a dog go into the emplacement, so he didn't throw the grenade because he didn't want to kill an innocent dog. Fortunately, it turned out that no German soldiers were there. Later, Mr. Schulz said, "I guess I fought a pretty civilized war."[231]

• In the telling of one World War II joke, the Nazi commandant of Paris ordered Pablo Picasso to appear before him. When Picasso was ushered into the commandant's presence, the commandant showed Picasso a reproduction of *Guernica*, the artist's anti-war mural that showed German bombers' destruction of Guernica during the Spanish

Civil War. The commandant asked Picasso, "Did you do that?" Picasso replied, "No. You did."[232]

• Author Quentin Crisp used to make a living as a nude model for art classes. During World War II, a bomb fell near where he was modeling. The art students dove for the floor and relative safety, but Mr. Crisp kept on posing.[233]

Weddings

• Many people, including straight people, love the characters of Alison Bechdel's comic strip *Dykes to Watch Out For*. At a wedding ceremony, one couple had a table set up to display objects representing people they wanted at the wedding, but who were not able to attend the ceremony. One of the items was a button of Mo, the central character in the comic strip (and the one based on its creator).[234]

• Stan Lee created the Fantastic Four with such characters as Richard Reed, who acquired the ability to stretch his body like rubber, and Sue Storm, who acquired the ability to become invisible and to create force fields. When the two characters got married in the comic book, Mr. Lee had artist Jack Kirby draw the two of them as characters attending the wedding.[235]

Work

• Bill Peet, author and illustrator of children's picture-books, worked many years for Walt Disney. He started out as an in-betweener — an artist who created the in-between drawings that resulted in a cartoon Donald Duck getting from one position to another — for example, lifting his arm in the air. However, he wanted to move up in the organization, so when the Disney artists were asked to create fantastic monsters for *Pinocchio*, he figured here was his chance, and so he drew many fantastic monsters and handed them in. Unfortunately, soon afterward another batch of Donald Duck in-between drawings were needed, and he went berserk, shouting, "NO MORE DUCKS! NO MORE LOUSY DUCKS!" — then he stalked out of his office. Later, he realized that he had left his jacket in his office, and the next morning he returned to pick it up. On his drawing table, he found an envelope waiting for him. Of course, he thought that it was a pink slip firing him; however, he discovered instead that the Disney company had liked his monster drawings, given him a bonus, and wanted him to quit creating in-betweens and instead report to the Story Department for *Pinocchio*.[236]

• As a young artist, Leonardo da Vinci painted a wooden shield for his father, Piero da Vinci. He went all out. After deciding to paint a fearsome creature on the shield, he dissected such animals as bats, crickets, insects, lizards, and snakes. He then used his knowledge of the parts of these animals to imaginatively create a monster that spit fire. Piero was impressed with the shield. He had intended to give it away as a gift, but after seeing it he gave his friend another, inexpensive shield — and he sold the shield that Leonardo had painted. As a young man, Leonardo had some notable skills. For example, he created stinkballs out of decomposing animal parts and fish guts. To entertain people, he used to create colorful flames by throwing red wine into a small container of boiling oil. Leonardo used his brain throughout his life and looked down on those who did not. He wrote, "How many people there are who could be described as mere channels for food." He wrote that such people produce "nothing but full privies."[237]

• When he was still very young, Jerry Butler's grandmother Artise (whom he called Grand Mo Lu) got him his first paying job as an artist. He had drawn a picture of Jesus, and she showed it to the people at the Baptist church they attended. They liked the drawing well enough to pay him to create a religious mural on the back of their baptismal pool. To pay for the mural, they took up a collection that netted him the seemingly astronomical sum of $140. Other religious people saw the mural, and they asked him to paint murals at their churches, too, paying him with what they took up in collections. In his 1998 book, *A Drawing in the Sand: A Story of African American Art*, Mr. Butler wrote that a couple of those murals still exist, but if he could, he would destroy them because his ability as an artist had grown so much since then.[238]

• Very early in his career, children's picture-book creator Ezra Jack Keats tried to get a job working for a miserly comic book artist as a cleanup and background man. He arrived to try out for the job with his own brushes because the comic book artist with the job didn't want him to ruin his brushes. In a poorly lit room, Mr. Keats worked for nearly an hour. The comic book artist then looked at his work, said, "This won't do," and told Mr. Keats that he owed him fifteen cents. Mr. Keats asked, "For what?" The comic book artist answered, "The ink." Mr. Keats was so tired and discouraged that he paid the fifteen cents. Fortunately, Mr. Keats became so successful in his career that he never had to charge a struggling artist fifteen cents for ink.[239]

• Julia Morgan was a woman who was an architect in the first half of the 20th century, a time when few women were working as architects. She often said, "Don't ever turn down a small job because you think it's beneath you." One of her smallest jobs was a two-room residence in Monterey, California, for a woman who became chair of the Young Women's Christian Association. Because the woman was pleased with her residence, she was instrumental in getting Ms. Morgan the job of designing several YWCAs — big jobs, all — across the country. (An even smaller job was when Ms. Morgan designed a tiny house for the daughters of her taxi driver to play in.)[240]

• During the Great Depression, the United States government created many jobs for its citizens. Among its jobs program was the Easel Project, which paid artists to create works of art. Many people are likely to regard such a program as a make-work program, with nothing significant resulting from it. Indeed, many of the paintings were sold to a plumber who was interested only in the canvas. He removed the canvas from the frames and used it in his plumbing work! However, some of the artists in the Easel Project, such as Romare

Bearden and Jacob Lawrence, became world-class (in addition to being African-American) artists.[241]

• Renaissance artist Michelangelo Buonarroti worked long and hard from 1508 to 1512 as he painted the ceiling of the Sistine Chapel. Often, he spent days and nights on the scaffolding without leaving, working as paint dripped onto his face and sleeping only inches from the ceiling. He slept in his clothes and his boots, and sometimes when he finally took off his boots, his skin came off with them. The ceiling is a masterpiece, but Pope Julius II became frustrated with the amount of time Michelangelo spent painting it. Sometimes, Pope Julius II came into the Sistine Chapel and yelled up at Michelangelo, "When will it be done?" Michelangelo always yelled back, "When it is done."[242]

• Country comedian Archie Campbell started out as an artist, and his talent came in handy. While serving in the United States Navy during World War II, he doodled while on duty, drawing several pictures of Donald Duck when he should have been working. His boss caught him in the act, but instead of bawling him out, he asked, "Can you do other things like that?" Mr. Campbell replied that he could, so his boss showed the doodles to a Lieutenant, and Mr. Campbell was put to work illustrating pamphlets for the Bureau of Personnel. In this job, he drew such things as Donald Duck pulling the wrong switch and getting an electrical shock.[243]

• African-American artist Palmer Hayden painted a work that illustrates how important the creation of art is to some people. *The Janitor Who Paints* (created about 1937) shows a janitor in his apartment — a super's apartment that is part of his pay as a janitor — working on a canvas while his wife and child pose for him. In the background is a clock displaying the time of 4:07 — showing that as soon as the artist's day job was done, he had rushed to his apartment and started painting. (Early in his career, Mr. Hayden made money to support his painting by cleaning other people's homes.)[244]

• Dale Messick was actually Dalía Messick, but she took a more masculine name to avoid having her work rejected by male editors and publishers simply because she was a woman. She created the comic strip *Brenda Starr*, and she kept on producing the strip even after she became pregnant, although she says that her workday became "throw up, draw *Brenda*, throw up, draw *Brenda*." She liked doing the comic strip and even named her daughter "Starr" and dyed her own hair red like that of her comic strip heroine.[245]

• *MAD* writer Dick DeBartolo and *MAD* artist Don Martin used to collaborate, but Mr. DeBartolo quickly noticed that when taking notes, Mr. Martin would sometimes change what he said. For example, when Mr. DeBartolo would write a musical satire, he would say something like, "In the opening panel, we see 50 girls in a line kicking …," but Mr. Martin would write, "Four girls in a line kicking." Mr. DeBartolo asked, "Why not 50?" Mr. Martin replied, "Because I have to draw them!"[246]

• During the Depression, Zero Mostel was employed as part of the Art Project, one of Franklin D. Roosevelt's programs to keep the people of the United States working. Mr. Mostel even taught for a while, although he was certainly an unconventional teacher (as are many art teachers). Once he grew hot during a class, so he went swimming in a nearby pool. When an administrator came by and asked Mr. Mostel what he was doing, he replied, "I'm studying water colors."[247]

• Charles M. Schulz, creator of the comic strip *Peanuts*, was a very careful worker. For the first four years he drew his comic strip, he never had a spelling error for his editor, Amy Lago, to find and correct. When he finally turned in a strip with a spelling error — he wrote "extention" instead of "extension" — Ms. Lago was so surprised that she checked a dictionary to make sure that "extention" was not an acceptable alternative spelling of "extension."[248]

• Like many illustrators of children's books, Pat Cummings frequently gives presentations in schools about her career. After one presentation, she received a letter from a girl who wrote that she had wanted to be an illustrator, but since Ms. Cummings had revealed how much work it was, she now wanted to be a lawyer.[249]

• Pablo Picasso lived until the age of 91, and he created works of art until the end of his life, leaving behind a prodigious amount of art. He created more than 15,000 paintings, as well as creating ceramics, drawings, prints, and sculptures. From the time he was eight years old, he averaged one work of art per day![250]

Appendix A: Bibliography

Addiss, Stephen, and G. Cameron Hurst III. *Samurai Painters*. Tokyo: Kodansha International, Ltd., 1983.

Alderson, Brian. *Ezra Jack Keats: Artist and Picture-Book Maker*. Gretna, LA: Pelican Publishing Co., Inc., 1994.

Aronson, Marc. *Art Attack: A Short Cultural History of the Avant-Garde*. New York: Clarion Books, 1998.

Bailey, Paul, editor. *The Stately Homo: A Celebration of the Life of Quentin Crisp*. London: Bantam Press, 2000.

Barreca, Regina, editor. *New Perspectives on Women and Comedy*. Philadelphia, PA: Gordon and Breach, 1992.

Barter, James. *Artists of the Renaissance*. San Diego, CA: Lucent Books, 1999.

Bechdel, Alison. *The Indelible Alison Bechdel: Confessions, Comix, and Miscellaneous Dykes to Watch Out For*. Ithaca, NY: Firebrand Books, 1998.

Berenstain, Stan and Jan. *Down a Sunny Dirt Road: An Autobiography*. New York: Random House, 2002.

Berman, Avis. *James McNeill Whistler*. New York: Harry N. Abrams, Inc., 1993.

Biggers, Don Hampton. *Buffalo Guns & Barbed Wire*. Lubbock, TX: Texas Tech University Press, 1991.

Billings, Henry and Melissa. *Eccentrics: 21 Stories of Unusual and Remarkable People*. Providence, RI: Jamestown Publishers, 1987.

Biracree, Tom. *Grandma Moses*. New York: Chelsea House Publishers, 1989.

Bolden, Tonya. *Wake Up Our Souls: A Celebration of Black American Artists*. New York: Harry N. Abrams, Inc., 2004.

Brasch, Walter M., editor. *ZIM: The Autobiography of Eugene Zimmerman*. Selinsgrove, PA: Susquehanna University Press; London and Toronto: Associated University Presses, 1988.

Brown, Jared. *Zero Mostel: A Biography*. New York: Atheneum, 1989.

Bryan III, J. *Merry Gentlemen (and One Lady)*. New York: Atheneum, 1985.

Burns, George. *Gracie: A Love Story*. New York: G.P. Putnam's Sons, 1988.

Butler, Jerry. *A Drawing in the Sand: A Story of African American Art*. Madison, WI: Zeno Press Children's Books, 1998.

Cain, Michael. *Mary Cassatt*. New York: Chelsea House Publishers, 1989.

Cain, Michael. *Louise Nevelson*. New York: Chelsea House Publishers, 1989.

Campbell, Archie. *Archie Campbell: An Autobiography*. With Ben Bryd. Memphis, TN: Memphis State University Press, 1981.

Camper, Jennifer. *subGURLZ*. San Francisco, CA: Cleis Press, 1999.

Caper, William. *Whoopi Goldberg: Comedian and Movie Star*. Springfield, NJ: Enslow Publications, Inc., 1999.

Caplin, Elliott. *Al Capp Remembered*. Bowling Green, OH: Bowling Green State University Popular Press, 1994.

Capp, Al. *My Well-Balanced Life on a Wooden Leg*. Santa Barbara, CA: John Daniel and Company, Publishers, 1991.

Clercq, Tanaquil Le. *The Ballet Cook Book*. New York: Stein and Day, Publishers, 1966.

Cornell, James. *Fakes, Frauds, and Phonies*. New York: Scholastic Book Services, 1973.

Cossi, Olga. *Edna Hibel: Her Life and Art*. Lowell, MA: Discovery Enterprises, Ltd., 1994.

Cowan, Lore and Maurice. *The Wit of the Jews*. Nashville, TN: Aurora Publishers, Limited, 1970.

Cranston, Toller. *Zero Tollerance*. With Martha Lowder Kimball. Toronto, Canada: McClelland and Stewart, Inc., 1997.

Cruz, Bárbara C. *José Clemente Orozco: Mexican Artist*. Berkeley Heights, NJ: Enslow Publications, Inc., 1998.

Cummings, Pat, compiler and editor. *Talking with Artists*. New York: Bradbury Press, 1992.

Cummings, Pat, compiler and editor. *Talking with Artists, Volume 2*. New York: Simon and Schuster Books for Young Readers, 1995.

Davis, Francis A. *Frank Lloyd Wright: Maverick Architect*. Minneapolis, MN: Lerner Publications Company, 1996.

DeBartolo, Dick. *Good Days and MAD*. New York: Thunder's Mouth Press, 1994.

Doonan, Simon. *Confessions of a Window Dresser*. New York: Penguin Studio, 1998.

Doonan, Simon. *Wacky Chicks: Life Lessons from Fearlessly Inappropriate and Fabulously Eccentric Women*. New York: Simon and Schuster, 2003.

Drucker, Hal, and Sid Lerner. *From the Desk Of*. Photographs by Sing-Si Schwartz. San Diego, CA: Harcourt Brace Jovanovich, Publishers, 1989.

Duggleby, John. *Story Painter: The Life of Jacob Lawrence*. San Francisco, CA: Chronicle Books, 1998.

Ebert, Roger; Curley, Daniel; and Jack Lane. *The Perfect London Walk*. Kansas City, MO: Andrews and McMeel, 1986.

Eichenbaum, Rose. *Masters of Movement: Portraits of America's Great Choreographers*. Washington, D.C.: Smithsonian Books, 2004.

Fisher, Barbara Milberg. *In Balanchine's Company: A Dancer's Memoir.* Middletown, CT: Wesleyan University Press, 2006.

Fletcher, Lynne Yamaguchi. *The First Gay Pope and Other Records.* Boston, MA: Alyson Publications, Inc., 1992.

Ford, Carin T. *Andy Warhol: Pioneer of Pop Art.* Berkeley Heights, NJ: Enslow Publications, Inc., 2001.

Ford, Carin T. *Dr. Seuss: Best-Loved Author.* Berkeley Heights, NJ: Enslow Publishers, Inc., 2002.

Ford, Michael Thomas. *It's Not Mean If It's True.* Los Angeles, CA: Alyson Books, 2000.

Ford, Michael Thomas. *Outspoken: Role Models from the Lesbian and Gay Community.* New York: Morrow Junior Books, 1998.

Furst, Herbert. *The New Anecdotes of Painters and Paintings.* London: The Bodley Head, Ltd., 1926.

Gaines, Ann Graham. *American Photographers: Capturing the Image.* Berkeley Heights, NJ: Enslow Publishers, Inc., 2002.

Gerler, William R. *Educator's Treasury of Humor for All Occasions.* West Nyack, NY: Parker Publishing Company, 1972.

Goldstein, Ernest. *The Statue* Abraham Lincoln: *A Masterpiece by Daniel Chester French.* Minneapolis, MN: Lerner Publications Company, 1997.

Gonzales, Doreen. *AIDS: Ten Stories of Courage.* Springfield, NJ: Enslow Publications, Inc., 1996.

Gonzales, Doreen. *Diego Rivera: His Art, His Life.* Berkeley Heights, NJ: Enslow Publications, Inc., 1996.

Greenberg, Jan, and Sandra Jordan. *The American Eye: Eleven Artists of the Twentieth Century.* New York: Delacorte Press, 1995.

Greenberg, Jan. *Romare Bearden: Collage of Memories.* New York: Harry N. Abrams, Inc., 2003.

Greenfeld, Howard. *Marc Chagall.* New York: Harry N. Abrams, Inc., 1990.

Greenfeld, Howard. *Paul Gauguin.* New York: Harry N. Abrams, Inc., 1993.

Hacker, Carlotta. *Great African Americans in The Arts.* New York: Crabtree Publishing Company, 1997.

Halliwell, Leslie. *The Filmgoer's Book of Quotes.* New Rochelle, NY: Arlington House, Publishers, 1973.

Hasday, Judy L. *Agnes de Mille.* Philadelphia, PA: Chelsea House Publishers, 2004.

Heiderstadt, Dorothy. *Painters of America.* New York: David McKay Company, Inc., 1970.

Henry, Lewis C. *Humorous Anecdotes About Famous People*. Garden City, NY: Halcyon House, 1948.

Hermann, Spring. *R.C. Gorman: Navaho Artist*. Springfield, NJ: Enslow Publications, Inc., 1995.

Humphrey, Laning, compiler. *The Humor of Music and Other Oddities in the Art*. Boston, MA: Crescendo Publishing Company, 1971.

Inge, M. Thomas, editor. *Dark Laughter: The Satiric Art of Oliver W. Harrington*. Jackson, MS: University Press of Mississippi, 1993.

Kahn, Albert E. *Days With Ulanova*. New York: Simon and Schuster, 1962.

Kandel, Bethany. *Trevor's Story*. Minneapolis, MN: Lerner Publications Company, 1997.

Keller, Emily. *Margaret Bourke-White: A Photographer's Life*. Minneapolis, MN: Lerner Publications Company, 1996.

Kinney, Jack. *Walt Disney and Other Assorted Characters: An Unauthorized Account of the Early Years at Disney's*. New York: Harmony Books, 1988.

Kovacs, Deborah, and James Preller. *Meet the Authors and Illustrators*. New York: Scholastic, Inc., 1991.

Krull, Kathleen. *Leonardo da Vinci*. New York: Viking, 2005.

Krull, Kathleen. *Lives of the Artists: Masterpieces, Messes (and What the Neighbors Thought)*. San Diego, CA: Harcourt Brace and Company, 1995.

Lassieur, Allison. *Leonardo da Vinci and the Renaissance in World History*. Berkeley Heights, NJ: Enslow Publications, Inc., 2000.

Ledbetter, Gordon T. *The Great Irish Tenor*. New York: Charles Scribner's Sons, 1977.

Lee, Stan, and George Mair. *Excelsior! The Amazing Life of Stan Lee*. New York: Fireside, 2002.

Leipold, L. Edmond. *Famous American Artists*. Minneapolis, MN: T.S. Denison and Company, Inc., 1969.

León, Vicki. *Uppity Women of Medieval Times*. New York: MJF Books, 1997.

Lessa, Christina. *Gymnastics Balancing Acts*. New York: Universe Publishing, 1997.

Lipman, Steve. *Laughter in Hell: The Use of Humor during the Holocaust*. Northvale, NJ: Jason Aronson, Inc., 1991.

Lyons, Mary E. *Starting Home: The Story of Horace Pippin, Painter*. New York: Charles Scribner's Sons, 1993.

Lyons, Mary E., editor. *Talking with Tebé: Clementine Hunter, Memory Artist*. Boston, MA: Houghton Mifflin Company, 1998.

Malone, Mary. *Maya Lin: Architect and Artist*. Berkeley Heights, NJ: Enslow Publications, Inc., 1995.

Marcus, Leonard S. *A Caldecott Celebration: Six Artists and Their Paths to the Caldecott Medal*. New York: Walker and Company, 1998.

Marcus, Leonard S. *Side By Side: Five Favorite Picture-Book Teams Go to Work*. New York: Walker and Company, 2001.

Marinacci, Barbara. *Leading Ladies: A Gallery of Famous Actresses*. New York: Dodd, Mead and Company, 1961.

Markova, Alicia. *Markova Remembers*. Boston, MA: Little, Brown and Company, 1986.

Massine, Léonide. *My Life in Ballet*. Edited by Phyllis Hartnoll and Robert Rubens. London: Macmillan and Co., Ltd., 1968.

McCann, Sean, compiler. *The Wit of Oscar Wilde*. New York: Barnes and Noble, Inc., 1969.

McKown, Robin. *The World of Mary Cassatt*. New York: Dell Publishing Co., Inc., 1972.

McLanathan, Richard. *Leonardo da Vinci*. New York: Harry N. Abrams, Inc., 1990.

McNeil, Legs, and Gillian McCain. *Please Kill Me: The Uncensored Oral History of Punk*. New York: Penguin Books, 1997.

McPhee, Nancy. *The Second Book of Insults*. Toronto, Canada: Van Nostrand Reinhold, Ltd., 1981.

Meryman, Richard. *Andrew Wyeth*. New York: Harry N. Abrams, Inc., 1991.

Meyer, Susan E. *Edgar Degas*. New York: Harry N. Abrams, Inc., 1994.

Meyer, Susan E. *Mary Cassatt*. New York: Harry N. Abrams, Inc., 1990.

Mingo, Jack. *The Juicy Parts*. New York: The Berkley Publishing Group, 1996.

Mingo, Jack, and Erin Barrett. *Lunchbox: From Comic Books to Cult TV and Beyond*. New York: HarperEntertainment, 2004.

Mullen, Tom. *Laughing Out Loud and Other Religious Experiences*. Waco, TX: Word Books, 1983.

Norkin, Sam. *Drawings, Stories: Theater, Opera, Ballet, Movies*. Portsmouth, NH: Heinemann, 1994.

O'Connor, Barbara. *Leonardo da Vinci: Renaissance Genius*. Minneapolis, MN: Carolrhoda Books, Inc., 2003.

Ohio University Emeriti Association, compilers. *Ohio University Recollections for the Bicentennial Anniversary: 1804-2004*. Athens, OH: Ohio University, 2004.

Old, Wendie C. *Louis Armstrong: King of Jazz*. Springfield, NJ: Enslow Publications, Inc., 1998.

Peet, Bill. *Bill Peet: An Autobiography*. Boston, MA: Houghton Mifflin Company, 1989.

Pflueger, Lynda. *Thomas Nast: Political Cartoonist*. Berkeley Heights, NJ: Enslow Publications, Inc., 2000.

Podgórecki, Adam. *The Tales of Si-tien*. London: Poets' and Painters' Press, 1973.

Primack, Ben, adapter and editor. *The Ben Hecht Show: Impolitic Observations from the Freest Thinker of 1950s Television*. Jefferson, NC: McFarland and Company, Inc., Publishers, 1993.

Rayner, William P. *Wise Women*. New York: St. Martin's Press, 1983.

Reidelbach, Maria. *Completely MAD: A History of the Comic Book and Magazine*. Boston, MA: Little, Brown and Company, 1991.

Robbins, Trina. *The Great Women Cartoonists*. New York: Watson-Guptill Publications, 2001.

Robbins, Trina, and Catherine Yronwode. *Women and the Comics*. [S.I.]: Eclipse Books, 1985.

Rodriguez-Hunter, Suzanne. *Found Meals of the Lost Generation*. Boston, MA: Faber and Faber, 1994.

Rosen, Michael J., editor. *Purr ... Children's Book Illustrators Brag About Their Cats*. San Diego, CA: Harcourt Brace and Company, 1996.

Rosen, Michael J., editor. *Speak! Children's Book Illustrators Brag About Their Dogs*. San Diego, CA: Harcourt Brace and Company, 1993.

Rubin, Susan Goldman. *Frank Lloyd Wright*. New York: Harry N. Abrams, Inc., 1994.

Samra, Cal and Rose, editors. *Holy Humor*. Colorado Springs, CO: WaterBrook Press, 1997.

Scherer, Barrymore Laurence. *Bravo! A Guide to Opera for the Perplexed*. New York: Dutton, 1996.

Schulz, Charles M. *Charlie Brown, Snoopy and Me*. With R. Smith Kiliper. Garden City, NY: Doubleday and Company, Inc., 1980.

Schuman, Michael A. *Charles M. Schulz: Cartoonist and Creator of* Peanuts. Berkeley Heights, NJ: Enslow Publishers, Inc., 2002.

Sellier, Marie. *Cézanne from A to Z*. New York: Peter Bedrick Books, 1995.

Shindler, Phyllis, collector. *Raise Your Glasses*. London: Judy Piatkus, Limited, 1988.

Simons II, Minot. *Women's Gymnastics: A History. Volume 1: 1966 to 1974*. Carmel, CA: Welwyn Publishing Company, 1995.

Smaridge, Norah. *Famous Author-Illustrators for Young People*. New York: Dodd, Mead and Company, 1973.

Smith, Bob. *Openly Bob*. New York: William Morrow and Company, Inc., 1997.

Smith, H. Allen. *The Compleat Practical Joker*. Garden City, NY: Doubleday and Company, Inc., 1953.

Sobol, Donald J. *Encyclopedia Brown's Book of the Wacky Outdoors*. New York: W. Morrow, 1987.

Sorel, Nancy Caldwell, and Edward Sorel. *First Encounters: A Book of Memorable Meetings*. New York: Alfred A. Knopf, 1994.

Steffens, Bradley, and Robyn M. Weaver. *Cartoonists*. San Diego, CA: Lucent Books, 2000.

Sufrin, Mark, *George Catlin: Painter of the Indian West*. New York: Atheneum, 1991.

Swisher, Clarice. *Pablo Picasso*. San Diego, CA: Lucent Books, 1995.

Tallchief, Maria. *Maria Tallchief: America's Prima Ballerina*. With Larry Kaplan. New York: Henry Holt and Company, 1997.

Terry, Walter. *Frontiers of Dance: The Life of Martha Graham*. New York: Thomas Y. Crowell Company, 1975.

Thomson, Peggy. *The Nine-Ton Cat: Behind the Scenes at an Art Museum*. With Barbara Moore. Edited by Carol Eron. Boston, MA: Houghton Mifflin Company, 1997.

Troy, Con. *Laugh with Hugh Troy, World's Greatest Practical Joker*. Wyomissing, PA: Trojan Books, 1983.

Tully, Jim. *A Dozen and One*. Hollywood, CA: Murray and Gee, Inc., Publishers, 1943.

Villella, Edward. *Prodigal Son: Dancing for Balanchine in a World of Pain and Magic*. With Larry Kaplan. New York: Simon and Schuster, Inc., 1992.

Von Habsburg, Geza. *Carl Fabergé*. New York: Harry N. Abrams, Inc., 1994.

Voskressenski, Alexei D., compiler and editor. *Cranks, Knaves, and Jokers of the Celestial*. Translated from the Chinese by Alexei Voskressenski and Vladimir Larin. Commack, NY: Nova Science Publishers, Inc., 1997.

Wadsworth, Ginger. *Julia Morgan: Architect of Dreams*. Minneapolis, MN: Lerner Publications Company, 1990.

Waldron, Ann. *Claude Monet*. New York: Harry N. Abrams, Inc., 1991.

Waldron, Ann. *Francisco Goya*. New York: Harry N. Abrams, Inc., 1992.

Warren, Roz, editor. *Dyke Strippers: Lesbian Cartoonists A to Z*. Pittsburgh, PA: Cleis Press, Inc., 1995.

Warren, Roz, editor. *Revolutionary Laughter: The World of Women Comics*. Freedom, CA: The Crossing Press, 1995.

Weidt, Maryann N. *Oh, the Places He Went: A Story About Dr. Seuss*. Minneapolis, MN: Carolrhoda Books, Inc., 1994.

Weissman, Ginny, and Coyne Steven Sanders. *The Dick Van Dyke Show*. New York: St. Martin's Press, 1993.

Wertheim, Lucy Carrington. *Adventures in Art*. London: Nicholson and Watson, 1947.

Whistler, James Abbott McNeill. *The Gentle Art of Making Enemies*. New York: Dover Publications, Inc., 1967.

Woolf, Vicki. *Dancing in the Vortex: The Story of Ida Rubinstein*. Australia: Harwood Academic Publishers, 2000.

Wulffson, Don L. *Amazing True Stories*. New York: Cobblehill Books, 1991.

Young, Robert. *A Personal Tour of Monticello*. Minneapolis, MN: Lerner Publications Company, 1999.

Appendix B: About the Author

It was a dark and stormy night. Suddenly a cry rang out, and on a hot summer night in 1954, Josephine, wife of Carl Bruce, gave birth to a boy — me. Unfortunately, this young married couple allowed Reuben Saturday, Josephine's brother, to name their first-born. Reuben, aka "The Joker," decided that Bruce was a nice name, so he decided to name me Bruce Bruce. I have gone by my middle name — David — ever since.

Being named Bruce David Bruce hasn't been all bad. Bank tellers remember me very quickly, so I don't often have to show an ID. It can be fun in charades, also. When I was a counselor as a teenager at Camp Echoing Hills in Warsaw, Ohio, a fellow counselor gave the signs for "sounds like" and "two words," then she pointed to a bruise on her leg twice. Bruise Bruise? Oh yeah, Bruce Bruce is the answer!

Uncle Reuben, by the way, gave me a haircut when I was in kindergarten. He cut my hair short and shaved a small bald spot on the back of my head. My mother wouldn't let me go to school until the bald spot grew out again.

Of all my brothers and sisters (six in all), I am the only transplant to Athens, Ohio. I was born in Newark, Ohio, and have lived all around Southeastern Ohio. However, I moved to Athens to go to Ohio University and have never left.

At Ohio U, I never could make up my mind whether to major in English or Philosophy, so I got a bachelor's degree with a double major in both areas and then I added a Master of Arts degree in English and a Master of Arts degree in Philosophy. Yes, I have my MAMA degree.

Currently, and for a long time to come (I eat fruits and veggies), I am spending my retirement writing books such as *Nadia Comaneci: Perfect 10*, *The Funniest People in Comedy*, *Homer's* Iliad: *A Retelling in Prose*, and *William Shakespeare's* Hamlet: *A Retelling in Prose*.

By the way, my sister Brenda Kennedy writes romances such as *A New Beginning* and *Shattered Dreams*.

Appendix C: Some Books by David Bruce

Anecdote Collections

250 Anecdotes About Opera
250 Anecdotes About Religion
250 Anecdotes About Religion: Volume 2
250 Music Anecdotes
Be a Work of Art: 250 Anecdotes and Stories
The Coolest People in Art: 250 Anecdotes
The Coolest People in the Arts: 250 Anecdotes
The Coolest People in Books: 250 Anecdotes
The Coolest People in Comedy: 250 Anecdotes
Create, Then Take a Break: 250 Anecdotes
Don't Fear the Reaper: 250 Anecdotes
The Funniest People in Art: 250 Anecdotes
The Funniest People in Books: 250 Anecdotes
The Funniest People in Books, Volume 2: 250 Anecdotes
The Funniest People in Books, Volume 3: 250 Anecdotes
The Funniest People in Comedy: 250 Anecdotes
The Funniest People in Dance: 250 Anecdotes
The Funniest People in Families: 250 Anecdotes
The Funniest People in Families, Volume 2: 250 Anecdotes
The Funniest People in Families, Volume 3: 250 Anecdotes
The Funniest People in Families, Volume 4: 250 Anecdotes
The Funniest People in Families, Volume 5: 250 Anecdotes
The Funniest People in Families, Volume 6: 250 Anecdotes
The Funniest People in Movies: 250 Anecdotes
The Funniest People in Music: 250 Anecdotes
The Funniest People in Music, Volume 2: 250 Anecdotes
The Funniest People in Music, Volume 3: 250 Anecdotes
The Funniest People in Neighborhoods: 250 Anecdotes
The Funniest People in Relationships: 250 Anecdotes
The Funniest People in Sports: 250 Anecdotes
The Funniest People in Sports, Volume 2: 250 Anecdotes
The Funniest People in Television and Radio: 250 Anecdotes
The Funniest People in Theater: 250 Anecdotes

The Funniest People Who Live Life: 250 Anecdotes
The Funniest People Who Live Life, Volume 2: 250 Anecdotes
The Kindest People Who Do Good Deeds, Volume 1: 250 Anecdotes
The Kindest People Who Do Good Deeds, Volume 2: 250 Anecdotes
Maximum Cool: 250 Anecdotes
The Most Interesting People in Movies: 250 Anecdotes
The Most Interesting People in Politics and History: 250 Anecdotes
The Most Interesting People in Politics and History, Volume 2: 250 Anecdotes
The Most Interesting People in Politics and History, Volume 3: 250 Anecdotes
The Most Interesting People in Religion: 250 Anecdotes
The Most Interesting People in Sports: 250 Anecdotes
The Most Interesting People Who Live Life: 250 Anecdotes
The Most Interesting People Who Live Life, Volume 2: 250 Anecdotes
Reality is Fabulous: 250 Anecdotes and Stories
Resist Psychic Death: 250 Anecdotes
Seize the Day: 250 Anecdotes and Storie

[1] Source: Mikhaela B. Reid, "Can't Make a Decision, Ladies? Call Bill Napoli." 13 April 2006 < https://stephaniemcmillan.org/in-these-times-interview-abortion-rights-comic/ >.

[2] Source: Simon Doonan, *Wacky Chicks*, p. 43.

[3] Source: Marc Aronson, *Art Attack: A Short Cultural History of the Avant-Garde*, pp. 154, 158.

[4] Source: Roz Warren, editor, *Dyke Strippers: Lesbian Cartoonists A to Z*, p. 135.

[5] Source: Carin T. Ford, *Dr. Seuss: Best-Loved Author*, pp. 7-8.

[6] Source: Simon Doonan, *Confessions of a Window Dresser*, p. 191.

[7] Source: Henry and Melissa Billings, *Eccentrics: 21 Stories of Unusual and Remarkable People*, pp. 98-100.

[8] Source: Roger Ebert, "'Crumb': How Comic Kept On Truckin'." 28 May 1995 < https://www.rogerebert.com/interviews/crumb-how-comic-kept-on-truckin >.

[9] Source: Nancy McPhee, *The Second Book of Insults*, p. 118.

[10] Source: Maryann N. Weidt, *Oh, the Places He Went: A Story About Dr. Seuss*, p. 48.

[11] Source: Lynne Yamaguchi Fletcher, *The First Gay Pope and Other Records*, pp. 42, 46.

[12] Source: Doreen Gonzales, *AIDS: Ten Stories of Courage*, p. 48.

[13] Source: Michael J. Rosen, editor, *Purr ... Children's Book Illustrators Brag About Their Cats*, p. 42.

[14] Source: Spring Hermann, *R.C. Gorman: Navaho Artist*, pp. 77-78.

[15] Source: Leonard S. Marcus, *A Caldecott Celebration: Six Artists and Their Paths to the Caldecott Medal*, p. 8.

[16] Source: Michael J. Rosen, editor, *Speak! Children's Book Illustrators Brag About Their Dogs*, p. 26.

[17] Source: Carin T. Ford, *Dr. Seuss: Best-Loved Author*, p. 42.

[18] Source: Dorothy Heiderstadt, *Painters of America*, p. 4.

[19] Source: Bob Smith, *Openly Bob*, p. 45.

[20] Source: Ginger Wadsworth, *Julia Morgan: Architect of Dreams*, p. 43.

[21] Source: Susan Goldman Rubin, *Frank Lloyd Wright*, pp. 53, 67-68.

[22] Source: Robert Young, *A Personal Tour of Monticello*, pp. 36-37.

[23] Source: Francis A. Davis, *Frank Lloyd Wright: Maverick Architect*, p. 87.

[24] Source: Leonard S. Marcus, *A Caldecott Celebration: Six Artists and Their Paths to the Caldecott Medal*, p. 14.

[25] Source: Alison Bechdel, *The Indelible Alison Bechdel*, p. 62.

[26] Source: William Caper, *Whoopi Goldberg: Comedian and Movie Star*, pp. 51-52.

[27] Source: Barrymore Laurence Scherer, *Bravo! A Guide to Opera for the Perplexed*, p. 46.

[28] Source: Sam Norkin, *Drawings, Stories*, p. 21.

[29] Source: Jennifer Camper, *subGURLZ*, back cover.

[30] Source: Bradley Steffens and Robyn M. Weaver, *Cartoonists*, p. 48.

[31] Source: Regina Barreca, editor, *New Perspectives on Women and Comedy*, p. 76.

[32] Source: Tom Mullen, *Laughing Out Loud and Other Religious Experiences*, p. 6.

[33] Source: Lewis C. Henry, *Humorous Anecdotes About Famous People*, p. 28.

[34] Source: Richard Meryman, *Andrew Wyeth*, pp. 17-18, 21.

[35] Source: Bill Peet, *Bill Peet: An Autobiography*, pp. 129-130.

[36] Source: Jerry Butler, *A Drawing in the Sand: A Story of African American Art*, pp. 8-10.

[37] Source: Stan and Jan Berenstain, *Down a Sunny Dirt Road*, p. 5.

[38] Source: Maryann N. Weidt, *Oh, the Places He Went: A Story About Dr. Seuss*, p. 29.

[39] Source: Brian Alderson, *Ezra Jack Keats: Artist and Picture-Book Maker*, pp. 188, 190.

[40] Source: Spring Hermann, *R.C. Gorman: Navaho Artist*, p. 15.

[41] Source: Emily Keller, *Margaret Bourke-White: A Photographer's Life*, p. 10.

[42] Source: Kathleen Krull, *Lives of the Artists*, p. 49.

[43] Source: James Barter, *Artists of the Renaissance*, p. 21.

[44] Source: Susan E. Meyer, *Mary Cassatt*, p. 61.

[45] Source: Bethany Kandel, *Trevor's Story*, p. 21.

[46] Source: Lynda Pflueger, *Thomas Nast: Political Cartoonist*, pp. 100, 102.

[47] Source: Charles M. Schulz, *Charlie Brown, Snoopy and Me*, p. 75.

[48] Source: Emily Keller, *Margaret Bourke-White: A Photographer's Life*, p. 35.

[49] Source: Suzanne Rodriguez-Hunter, *Found Meals of the Lost Generation*, p. 13.

[50] Source: Doreen Gonzales, *Diego Rivera: His Art, His Life*, pp. 40-41.

[51] Source: Alexei D. Voskressenski, compiler and editor, *Cranks, Knaves, and Jokers of the Celestial*, p. 26.

[52] Source: Laning Humphrey, compiler, *The Humor of Music and Other Oddities in the Art*, pp. 92-93.

[53] Source: Lore and Maurice Cowan, *The Wit of the Jews*, p. 15.

[54] Source: Susan E. Meyer, *Edgar Degas*, p. 87.

[55] Source: Jack Mingo and Erin Barrett, *Lunchbox*, p. 135.

[56] Source: William R. Gerler, *Educator's Treasury of Humor for All Occasions*, p. 124.

[57] Source: Stan Lee and George Mair, *Excelsior! The Amazing Life of Stan Lee*, p. 154.

[58] Source: Maria Tallchief, *Maria Tallchief: America's Prima Ballerina*, pp. 59-60.

[59] Source: Alicia Markova, *Markova Remembers*, p. 100.

[60] Source: Allison Lassieur, *Leonardo da Vinci and the Renaissance in World History*, p. 50.

[61] Source: Doreen Gonzales, *AIDS: Ten Stories of Courage*, pp. 48-49, 51.

[62] Source: Sean McCann, compiler, *The Wit of Oscar Wilde*, pp. 81-82.

[63] Source: Legs McNeil and Gillian McCain, *Please Kill Me*, p. 23.

[64] Source: Jack Mingo, *The Juicy Parts*, p. 79.

[65] Source: James Cornell, *Fakes, Frauds, and Phonies*, pp. 57-59.

[66] Source: Walter M. Brasch, editor, *ZIM: The Autobiography of Eugene Zimmerman*, p. 72.

[67] Source: Roger Ebert, "Movie Buffs Loved It Wilder." 29 March 2002 <www.suntimes.com/output/eb-feature/cst-ftr-wild29.html>.

[68] Source: Adam Podgórecki, *The Tales of Si-tien*, p. 24.

[69] Source: Tom Biracree, *Grandma Moses*, p. 91.

[70] Source: Martin Gayford, "Elitist snob, doyen of art critics." *The Telegraph*. 15 October 2006 <http://www.telegraph.co.uk/arts/main.jhtml;jsessionid=JFTBX3C03M2B1QFIQMGCFGGAVCBQUIV0?xml=/arts/2006/10/15/bohug207.xml>.

[71] Source: James Abbott McNeill Whistler, *The Gentle Art of Making Enemies*, p. 66.

[72] Source: Avis Berman, *James McNeill Whistler*, p. 8.

[73] Source: Howard Greenfeld, *Paul Gauguin*, p. 44.

[74] Source: Albert E. Kahn, *Days With Ulanova*, p. 118.

[75] Source: Don L. Wulffson, *Amazing True Stories*, pp. 57-59.

[76] Source: Tom Biracree, *Grandma Moses*, pp. 94-95.

[77] Source: Léonide Massine, *My Life in Ballet*, pp. 58-59.

[78] Source: Roger Ebert and Daniel Curley, *The Perfect London Walk*, p. 102.

[79] Source: Minot Simons II, *Women's Gymnastics: A History. Volume 1: 1966 to 1974*, pp. 265-266.

[80] Source: Jan Greenberg and Sandra Jordan, *The American Eye: Eleven Artists of the Twentieth Century*, pp. 79-80.

[81] Source: Barbara O'Connor, *Leonardo da Vinci: Renaissance Genius*, pp. 50-51, 77.

[82] Source: Toller Cranston, *Zero Tollerance*, p. 7.

[83] Source: Howard Greenfield, *Marc Chagall*, pp. 24-25, 27.

[84] Source: Barbara Milberg Fisher, *In Balanchine's Company: A Dancer's Memoir*, pp. 80, 83.

[85] Source: Stan and Jan Berenstain, *Down a Sunny Dirt Road*, p. 35.

[86] Source: Susan Goldman Rubin, *Frank Lloyd Wright*, p. 47.

[87] Source: John Duggleby, *Story Painter: The Life of Jacob Lawrence*, p. 47.

[88] Source: Avis Berman, *James McNeill Whistler*, p. 18.

[89] Source: Deborah Kovacs and James Preller, *Meet the Authors and Illustrators*, p. 66.

[90] Source: Maria Reidelbach, *Completely MAD*, p. 190.

[91] Source: Léonide Massine, *My Life in Ballet*, p. 106.

[92] Source: Con Troy, *Laugh with Hugh Troy*, p. 88.

[93] Source: Michael Cain, *Mary Cassatt*, p. 90.

[94] Source: Michael Cain, *Louise Nevelson*, p. 60.

[95] Source: Carlotta Hacker, *Great African Americans in The Arts*, pp. 22, 24, 27.

[96] Source: Susan E. Meyer, *Mary Cassatt*, pp. 88-89.

[97] Source: William P. Rayner, *Wise Women*, p. 3.

[98] Source: Ben Primack, adapter and editor, *The Ben Hecht Show*, pp. 59-60.

[99] Source: Richard Meryman, *Andrew Wyeth*, pp. 64-65.

[100] Source: Rose Eichenbaum, *Masters of Movement: Portraits of America's Great Choreographers*, p. 30.

[101] Source: Jared Neumark, "The Gnome Man." 13 September 2006 <http://charlotte.creativeloafing.com/gyrobase/Content?oid=oid%3A74398>.

[102] Source: Francis A. Davis, *Frank Lloyd Wright: Maverick Architect*, p. 17.

[103] Source: James Cornell, *Fakes, Frauds, and Phonies*, pp. 94-97.

[104] Source: Leonard S. Marcus, *Side By Side: Five Favorite Picture-Book Teams Go to Work*, pp. 21, 24-25.

[105] Source: Michael Thomas Ford, *Outspoken*, p. 18.

[106] Source: Michael Thomas Ford, *It's Not Mean If It's True*, p. 172.

[107] Source: Phyllis Shindler, collector, *Raise Your Glasses*, p. 33.

[108] Source: Michael J. Rosen, editor, *Speak! Children's Book Illustrators Brag About Their Dogs*, p. 37.

[109] Source: Deborah Kovacs and James Preller, *Meet the Authors and Illustrators*, p. 56.

[110] Source: Cal and Rose Samra, *Holy Humor*, pp. 22-23.

[111] Source: Don L. Wulffson, *Amazing True Stories*, p. 56.

[112] Source: William R. Gerler, *Educator's Treasury of Humor for All Occasions*, p. 46.

[113] Source: Ohio University Emeriti Association, compilers, *Ohio University Recollections for the Bicentennial Anniversary: 1804-2004*, pp. 59-60.

[114] Source: M. Thomas Inge, editor, *Dark Laughter*, p. xiii.

[115] Source: Pat Cummings, compiler and editor, *Talking with Artists*, p. 10.

[116] Source: Peggy Thomson, *The Nine-Ton Cat: Behind the Scenes at an Art Museum*, pp. 32-33, 35, 74-75.

[117] Source: Ann Graham Gaines, *American Photographers: Capturing the Image*, pp. 30-32.

[118] Source: Ernest Goldstein, *The Statue* Abraham Lincoln: *A Masterpiece by Daniel Chester French*, pp. 53-55, 57.

[119] Source: Bárbara C. Cruz, *José Clemente Orozco: Mexican Artist*, pp. 39-40, 73.

[120] Source: Al Capp, *My Well-Balanced Life on a Wooden Leg*, pp. 36, 38-39.

[121] Source: Mary E. Lyons, *Starting Home: The Story of Horace Pippin, Painter*, pp. 1-2.

[122] Source: Olga Cossi, *Edna Hibel: Her Life and Art*, p. 25.

[123] Source: Michael Cain, *Mary Cassatt*, pp. 39, 44, 84-85.

[124] Source: Jared Brown, *Zero Mostel: A Biography*, p. 6.

[125] Source: Judy L. Hasday, *Agnes de Mille*, p. 71.

[126] Source: Lynda Pflueger, *Thomas Nast: Political Cartoonist*, pp. 6, 8, 10.

[127] Source: Geza Von Habsburg, *Carl Fabergé*, pp. 32-33, 38-39.

[128] Source: Archie Campbell, *Archie Campbell: An Autobiography*, pp. 149-152.

[129] Source: Lucy Carrington Wertheim, *Adventure in Art*, p. 30.

[130] Source: Olga Cossi, *Edna Hibel: Her Life and Art*, pp. 22-23.

[131] Source: Carin T. Ford, *Andy Warhol: Pioneer of Pop Art*, pp. 6-7.

[132] Source: James Abbott McNeill Whistler, *The Gentle Art of Making Enemies*, p. 5.

[133] Source: Carlotta Hacker, *Great African Americans in The Arts*, p. 42. Also: <http://cghs.dade.k12.fl.us/african-american/reconstruct/tanner.htm>.

[134] Source: Jan Greenberg and Sandra Jordan, *The American Eye: Eleven Artists of the Twentieth Century*, p. 54.

[135] Source: Kathleen Krull, *Lives of the Artists*, pp. 34-35.

[136] Source: Suzanne Rodriguez-Hunter, *Found Meals of the Lost Generation*, p. 3.

[137] Source: Herbert Furst, *The New Anecdotes of Painters and Paintings*, pp. 23-24.

[138] Source: Carin T. Ford, *Andy Warhol: Pioneer of Pop Art*, p. 8.

[139] Source: Nancy McPhee, *The Second Book of Insults*, pp. 53-54.

[140] Source: Robin McKown, *The World of Mary Cassatt*, p. 159.

[141] Source: Leslie Halliwell, *The Filmgoer's Book of Quotes*, p. 122.

[142] Source: Jack Mingo, *The Juicy Parts*, p. 79.

[143] Source: Jim Tully, *A Dozen and One*, p. 129.

[144] Source: Lucy Carrington Wertheim, *Adventure in Art*, pp. 57-58.

[145] Source: Bradley Steffens and Robyn M. Weaver, *Cartoonists*, pp. 60, 62.

[146] Source: Simon Doonan, *Confessions of a Window Dresser*, p. 15.

[147] Source: Mark Sufrin, *George Catlin: Painter of the Indian West*, pp. 47, 145. Also: Don Hampton Biggers, *Buffalo Guns & Barbed Wire*, pp. 101-102.

[148] Source: Geza Von Habsburg, *Carl Fabergé*, pp. 58, 66.

[149] Source: Peggy Thomson, *The Nine-Ton Cat: Behind the Scenes at an Art Museum*, p. 79.

[150] Source: Wendie C. Old, *Louis Armstrong: King of Jazz*, p. 96.

[151] Source: Legs McNeil and Gillian McCain, *Please Kill Me*, p. 173.

[152] Source: Trina Robbins and Catherine Yronwode, *Women and the Comics*, pp. 36, 40.

[153] Source: Charles M. Schulz, *Charlie Brown, Snoopy and Me*, pp. 40-41.

[154] Source: Trina Robbins, *The Great Women Cartoonists*, p. 115.

[155] Source: J. Bryan III, *Merry Gentlemen (and One Lady)*, p. 56. Also: "Neysa McMein" <http://en.wikipedia.org/wiki/Neysa_Mcmein>.

[156] Source: Susan E. Meyer, *Edgar Degas*, pp. 65-66, 85.

[157] Source: Hal Drucker and Sid Lerner, *From the Desk Of*, p. 32.

[158] Source: Doreen Gonzales, *Diego Rivera: His Art, His Life*, pp. 34-35.

[159] Source: Tanaquil Le Clercq, *The Ballet Cook Book*, pp. 38-39.

[160] Source: Ann Waldron, *Claude Monet*, p. 55.

[161] Source: Roger Ebert, "A New Take on Hearst Saga." 24 April 2002 <www.suntimes.com/output/eb-feature/cst-ftr-lead24.html>.

[162] Source: Mary E. Lyons, editor, *Talking with Tebé: Clementine Hunter, Memory Artist*, p. 31.

[163] Source: Allison Lassieur, *Leonardo da Vinci and the Renaissance in World History*, p. 49.

[164] Source: Marie Sellier, *Cézanne from A to Z*, pp. 8, 26-27.

[165] Source: Robin McKown, *The World of Mary Cassatt*, p. 127.

[166] Source: Howard Greenfeld, *Paul Gauguin*, pp. 46-47.

[167] Source: Vicki León, *Uppity Women of Medieval Times*, p. 99.

[168] Source: Mary E. Lyons, *Starting Home: The Story of Horace Pippin, Painter*, pp. 19, 21, 28-29.

[169] Source: Bárbara C. Cruz, *José Clemente Orozco: Mexican Artist*, pp. 8-9, 98, 105.

[170] Source: Al Capp, *My Well-Balanced Life on a Wooden Leg*, p. 42.

[171] Source: Nancy Caldwell Sorel and Edward Sorel, *First Encounters*, p. 49.

[172] Source: Donald J. Sobol, *Encyclopedia Brown's Book of the Wacky Outdoors*, pp. 55-57.

[173] Source: Albert E. Kahn, *Days With Ulanova*, p. xii.

[174] Source: Maria Reidelbach, *Completely MAD*, p. 54.

[175] Source: Rose Eichenbaum, *Masters of Movement: Portraits of America's Great Choreographers*, p. 225.

[176] Source: Christina Lessa, *Gymnastics Balancing Acts*, p. 5.

[177] Source: Walter Terry, *Frontiers of Dance: The Life of Martha Graham*, p. 148.

[178] Source: Gordon T. Ledbetter, *The Great Irish Tenor*, p. 9.

[179] Source: William P. Rayner, *Wise Women*, p. 7.

[180] Source: L. Edmond Leipold, *Famous American Artists*, p. 20.

[181] Source: Marie Sellier, *Cézanne from A to Z*, p. 38.

[182] Source: Vicki Woolf, *Dancing in the Vortex: The Story of Ida Rubinstein*, p. 46.

[183] Source: Barbara Marinacci, *Leading Ladies: A Gallery of Famous Actresses*, p. 52.

[184] Source: Jack Kinney, *Walt Disney and Other Assorted Characters*, p. 56.

[185] Source: H. Allen Smith, *The Compleat Practical Joker*, pp. 40-41.

[186] Source: Michael J. Rosen, editor, *Purr ... Children's Book Illustrators Brag About Their Cats*, p. 6.

[187] Source: J. Bryan III, *Merry Gentlemen (and One Lady)*, p. 274.

[188] Source: Jan Greenberg, *Romare Bearden: Collage of Memories*, pp. 15-16, 26.

[189] Source: M. Thomas Inge, editor, *Dark Laughter*, p. xi.

[190] Source: Trina Robbins and Catherine Yronwode, *Women and the Comics*, p. 78.

[191] Source: Tonya Bolden, *Wake Up Our Souls*, pp. 22-23. Also: "Edward Mitchell Bannister." Accessed 25 November 2007 <http://en.wikipedia.org/wiki/Edward_Mitchell_Bannister>.

[192] Source: Mary Malone, *Maya Lin: Architect and Artist*, p. 28.

[193] Source: Jan Greenberg, *Romare Bearden: Collage of Memories*, pp. 28-29.

[194] Source: Mary E. Lyons, editor, *Talking with Tebé: Clementine Hunter, Memory Artist*, pp. 26, 31, 41-42, 44-45.

[195] Source: Dorothy Heiderstadt, *Painters of America*, pp. 112, 118.

[196] Source: Adam Podgórecki, *The Tales of Si-tien*, pp. 18-19.

[197] Source: Michael Cain, *Louise Nevelson*, pp. 88-89.

[198] Source: Richard McLanathan, *Leonardo da Vinci*, pp. 78-79.

[199] Source: Elliott Caplin, *Al Capp Remembered*, p. 71.

[200] Source: Leonard S. Marcus, *Side By Side: Five Favorite Picture-Book Teams Go to Work*, pp. 15-16.

[201] Source: Norah Smaridge, *Famous Author-Illustrators for Young People*, pp. 106, 109.

[202] Source: Herbert Furst, *The New Anecdotes of Painters and Paintings*, pp. 46-47.

[203] Source: Roz Warren, editor, *Revolutionary Laughter*, pp. 281-282.

[204] Source: Ann Waldron, *Claude Monet*, p. 76.

[205] Source: Ann Waldron, *Francisco Goya*, p. 44.

[206] Source: Edward Villella, *Prodigal Son: Dancing for Balanchine in a World of Pain and Magic*, p. 79.

[207] Source: Richard McLanathan, *Leonardo da Vinci*, p. 28.

[208] Source: Stephen Addiss and G. Cameron Hurst III, *Samurai Painters*, p. 48.

[209] Source: Elliott Caplin, *Al Capp Remembered*, pp. 91-94.

[210] Source: Con Troy, *Laugh with Hugh Troy*, pp. 95-96.

[211] Source: L. Edmond Leipold, *Famous American Artists*, p. 45.

[212] Source: Mary Malone, *Maya Lin: Architect and Artist*, pp. 12, 29, 32, 38, 41, 43.

[213] Source: Ernest Goldstein, *The Statue* Abraham Lincoln: *A Masterpiece by Daniel Chester French*, pp. 18, 27-29.

[214] Source: Clarice Swisher, *Pablo Picasso*, p. 72. Also: "Bull's Head." Wikipedia

[215] Source: Marc Aronson, *Art Attack: A Short Cultural History of the Avant-Garde*, p. 94.

[216] Source: George Burns, *Gracie: A Love Story*, pp. 180-182.

[217] Source: Norah Smaridge, *Famous Author-Illustrators for Young People*, p. 95.

[218] Source: Jack Kinney, *Walt Disney and Other Assorted Characters*, p. 69.

[219] Source: Ginny Weissman and Coyne Steven Sanders, *The Dick Van Dyke Show*, p. 46.

[220] Source: Jack Mingo and Erin Barrett, *Lunchbox*, p. 15.

[221] Source: Walter M. Brasch, editor, *ZIM: The Autobiography of Eugene Zimmerman*, p. 70.

[222] Source: Sam Norkin, *Drawings, Stories*, p. 164.

[223] Source: Pat Cummings, compiler and editor, *Talking with Artists, Volume 2*, p. 35.

[224] Source: Tanaquil Le Clercq, *The Ballet Cook Book*, p. 283.

[225] Source: H. Allen Smith, *The Compleat Practical Joker*, p. 29.

[226] Source: Ann Waldron, *Francisco Goya*, p. 86.

[227] Source: Toller Cranston, *Zero Tollerance*, pp. 248-249.

[228] Source: Dick DeBartolo, *Good Days and MAD*, p. 164.

[229] Source: Howard Greenfield, *Marc Chagall*, pp. 77, 79.

[230] Source: Ann Graham Gaines, *American Photographers: Capturing the Image*, pp. 19-22.

[231] Source: Michael A. Schuman, *Charles M. Schulz*, pp. 25-27.

[232] Source: Steve Lipman, *Laughter in Hell*, p. 85.

[233] Source: Paul Bailey, editor, *The Stately Homo: A Celebration of the Life of Quentin Crisp*, p. 100.

[234] Source: Alison Bechdel, *The Indelible Alison Bechdel*, p. 212.

[235] Source: Stan Lee and George Mair, *Excelsior! The Amazing Life of Stan Lee*, p. 118.

[236] Source: Bill Peet, *Bill Peet: An Autobiography*, pp. 88-94.

[237] Source: Kathleen Krull, *Leonardo da Vinci*, pp. 28, 30-31, 39.

[238] Source: Jerry Butler, *A Drawing in the Sand: A Story of African American Art*, pp. 22-23.

[239] Source: Brian Alderson, *Ezra Jack Keats: Artist and Picture-Book Maker*, p. 28.

[240] Source: Ginger Wadsworth, *Julia Morgan: Architect of Dreams*, pp. 28, 58.

[241] Source: John Duggleby, *Story Painter: The Life of Jacob Lawrence*, pp. 29-30.

[242] Source: James Barter, *Artists of the Renaissance*, pp. 76-77.

[243] Source: Archie Campbell, *Archie Campbell: An Autobiography*, p. 76.

[244] Source: Tonya Bolden, *Wake Up Our Souls*, pp. 46-47.

[245] Source: Trina Robbins, *The Great Women Cartoonists*, pp. 49-50, 62.

[246] Source: Dick DeBartolo, *Good Days and MAD*, p. 159.

[247] Source: Jared Brown, *Zero Mostel: A Biography*, p. 18.

[248] Source: Michael A. Schuman, *Charles M. Schulz*, p. 100.

[249] Source: Pat Cummings, compiler and editor, *Talking with Artists*, p. 9.

[250] Source: Clarice Swisher, *Pablo Picasso*, p. 94.

www.ingramcontent.com/pod-product-compliance
Lightning Source LLC
Chambersburg PA
CBHW051239160726
47994CB00002B/946